EDITORIAL RESEARCH REPORTS ON

Modern Man

Published by Congressional Quarterly, Inc.
1735 K Street, N.W.
Washington, D.C. 20006

About the Cover

We are indebted to Helaine Blumenfeld, an American now living in Cambridge, England, for permission to photograph and reproduce two of her sculptures, cast in 1970 in polished bronze. Mrs. Blumenfeld has had showings in New York, Paris and Vienna. Editorial Research Reports staff artist Howard Chapman is responsible for the overall design and execution of the cover.

Published January 1971

Library of Congress Catalogue Card Number 71-148403
Standard Book No. 87187-015-0

Editorial Research Reports
Editor Emeritus, Richard M. Boeckel
Editor, William B. Dickinson, Jr.
Associate Editor for Reports, Hoyt Gimlin

Contents

FOREWORD

MODERN MAN and the complex society he has wrought are leading an uneasy coexistence. The advance into a super-industrial era has been so rapid that sometimes the machine rather than its maker seems to be in control. Moreover, the accelerative thrust is so great that technology feeds on itself, making more technology possible before people have had time to digest the first innovation.

Man, a creature of habit, can't seem to adapt readily to the charged pace of technological change. Social commentators must come up with a new vocabulary to describe the resulting illness. Alvin Toffler, for one, has used the term "future shock" —defined as "the dizzying disorientation brought on by the premature arrival of the future." He believes it may well be the most important disease of tomorrow.

A still worse diagnosis comes from Robert Jay Lifton, research professor of psychiatry at Yale Medical School. Lifton's theory, set forth in a new book, *Boundaries*, is that the atomic age has brought an end to man's sense of limits concerning his self-destructive potential. This has inaugurated an era in which man has little assurance of living on as a species. Hiroshima and Auschwitz are seen as symbols of the triumph of technological absurdity. Young people are left with an inner knowledge that their world is capable of exterminating itself. As a consequence, youth experiences a continuing anxiety related not so much to death itself as to an underlying terror of premature death and unfulfilled life.

* * * * *

WHAT HAPPENS to contemporary man when he becomes overwhelmed by the mad pace of technological change and the vision of impermanence that it implies? For one thing, we begin to fall victim to physical and psychic ills both as individuals and as a society. Youth becomes alienated, with some seeking a return to a simpler Thoreauvian existence while others turn in rage on the established institutions that seem to be respon-sible for putting the times out of joint. Older people retreat into the past, refusing to face up to changes that cannot be

i

reversed. Some conclude that the faith of their fathers has failed them and turn to tarot cards and horoscopes. A general resurgence of superstition and magic show that our yearning for the transcendent is taking us down strange—and possibly dangerous—paths.

The evidence seems overwhelming. Out of the womb of our post-atomic society have come consequences that threaten to alter the very nature of man and of his relation to the universe. Yet a casual reading of history should show that our plight is far from unique. One need only recall the series of scientific ideas and discoveries that shook the foundations of society half a millennium ago. Copernicus defied the authority of Aristotle, the Bible, and the church fathers when he propounded the theory that the sun, rather than the earth, was the central body around which the planets revolved. Man was no longer the center of God's universe! In an Age of Faith, the refuting of theological dogma proved devastating. Orthodoxy waged a last-ditch fight against the new heretics, and the civilized world was incarnadined in the resulting wars and inquisitions. Irrationality was triumphant—for a time.

* * * * *

BUT DISORGANIZED BEHAVIOR can be seen as part of an essential problem-solving process. Doctors who work with the mentally ill know that certain types of insanity can be good for an individual—if they lead to a cathartic experience that reorganizes the entire personality. Dr. Karl Menninger has described cases in which some of his patients suffer an acute mental disturbance "and then get well and then they get weller!...I mean they get better than they ever were." The same outcome may apply to society as a whole. If, as some observers think, we are undergoing a national nervous breakdown, the recovery may well set the stage for a new era of progress and enlightenment.

Such optimism is not likely to impress young people sunk in gloom and self-doubt as they watch the fabric of society come apart. The paradox of our contentious time is that the fiercest affirmations of life come from those closest to the grave. Historian Will Durant at the age of 83 felt sanguine enough to write (*The Lessons of History*, 1968): "If we take the long-range view and compare our modern existence, precarious, chaotic and murderous as it is, with the ignorance, superstition, violence and disease of primitive peoples, we do not come off quite forlorn....Some time ago a convention of morticians discussed the danger threatening their industry from the increasing tardiness of men in keeping their rendezvous with death. If undertakers are miserable, progress is real."

And Lewis Mumford, 75, concludes his *The Myth of the Machine*, Vol. II (1970), with the stirring injunction: "On the terms imposed by technocratic society, there is no hope for mankind except by 'going with' its plans for accelerated technological progress, even though man's vital organs will all be cannibalized in order to prolong the megamachine's meaningless existence. But for those of us who have thrown off the myth of the machine, the next move is ours: for the gates of the technocratic prison will open automatically, despite their rusty ancient hinges, as soon as we choose to walk out."

Modern man, in short, can recapture some of his lost innocence by insisting that moral and humanistic judgments be brought to bear on the application of his discoveries. If he does, we may see the dawn of a New Age of Reason. It is to that hope—and it is a real one—that the research reports in this volume are dedicated.

William B. Dickinson Jr.
Editor

November 1970
Washington, D.C.

THE NEW HUMANISM

by

Helen B. Shaffer

1 9 7 0
Nov. 4

THE NEW HUMANISM

M AN'S AGE-OLD search for the good life on earth is moving along new tracks as the 20th century approaches its last quarter. And the goal is more elusive than ever. Not only is technology leaping along at a bewildering pace, changing the physical conditions of life, but social institutions are becoming increasingly complex and remote from the individual's control. The idea is taking hold that what man has wrought, he has not always wrought for his own well-being. The result is a rising demand for more humane considerations in the making of fateful decisions that determine what kind of world modern man and his progeny must live in. Thus at the dawning of the "post-industrial" age, a new humanism is arising.

Much of the new humanism takes the form of protest against technological "progress." As culture critic William Braden puts it, there is "a humanistic revolt against technology, against the debatable form of affluence that technology has so far produced in this country, and indeed against the basic psychological, philosophical, and theological assumptions that underlie the technological impulse to manipulate the environment and thereby to dominate the universe." He added that "no less than the whole thrust of western civilization since at least the Renaissance and Reformation" is being called into question.[1]

As expressed by Prof. Charles A. Reich of the Yale Law School in his much-discussed new book, *The Greening of America* (1970), the revolt of youth—long hair, student protest, rock music, rejection of careers—is basically a repudiation of the "corporate state" and its web of impersonal institutions that determine the conditions of modern life. Young people, however, are not the only ones affected; among older Americans there is widespread disillusionment. Social reform and

[1] William Braden, *The Age of Aquarius: Technology and the Cultural Revolution* (1970), p. 5.

economic progress—the gods of yesteryear—have failed to produce a paradise on earth.

Not everyone can articulate the humanist complaint in terms that scholars and publicists of the movement do. But it is impossible to view the direction of American life without sensing a widespread desire for a more humane quality of life. It may well be indicative of a response to the current humanist criticism that President Nixon asked his new science adviser, Edward E. David, to concentrate on ways of using scientific research and discovery "for the benefit of the people."[2]

Response of Government to Humanist Concerns

Considerations of humane goals are evident in legislation dealing with the environment. Objectives are sometimes couched in Thoreau-like terms. A bill introduced in 1970 would establish a joint congressional committee to deal with environmental problems "in a manner to foster, promote, create and maintain conditions under which man and nature can exist in harmony." The National Environmental Policy Act of 1969, in setting policy goals for recycling depletable resources, called for the achievement of a balance between population and resource use "which will permit...a wide sharing of life's amenities." These measures reflect, in language at least, some of the aspirations of latter-day humanists.

The government remains a major target of humanist criticism, however. It has been noted that the government issues an annual economic report, replete with indicators of productivity, employment, inflation, investment, consumption, and the like. But it issues no report on the human condition of the American people. Similar indicators on the national health, the state of the environment, the degree and location of poverty, the costs and effects of crime, the richness of education and science and art—all these are absent but needed, according to the federal officials who wrote *Toward a Social Report* (1969) for the Department of Health, Education, and Welfare.

One of the authors of the report observed later: "No society in history has as yet made a coherent and unified effort to assess those factors that...help or hinder the individual citizen to establish a career commensurate with his abilities, or to live

---

[2] As David related to newsmen after meeting with the President at the White House, Aug. 19, 1970. David succeeded Lee A. DuBridge, a physicist, as presidential science adviser. See "Science and Society," *E.R.R.*, 1969 Vol. II, pp. 773-792.

a full and healthy life equal to his biological potential...and which suggest what a 'decent' physical and social environment ought to be." *Toward a Social Report* was described as the first step in doing so.[3]

That discontent is widespread in America seems to be a universal opinion. Reporting on its survey of the mood of the nation, *U.S. News & World Report* commented in the spring of 1970: "An atmosphere of discontent is spreading across America. It shows itself in many forms—frustration, vexation, defiance, anxiety, a brooding dissatisfaction with the way things are going in the world's richest and strongest nation."[4] Howard K. Smith, the television news commentator, wrote on "frustrated America" in the journal of the American Humanist Association: "We are tense, discontented, frustrated... easily angered over small things; we explode over big things and we are divided." It was all the more curious, he thought, because "basic conditions have never been more favorable than they are today."[5]

Dissatisfaction With Goals of Affluent Society

Sources of discontent are manifold. Leo Cherne, executive director of the Research Institute of America, attributes discontent to loss of faith that "every problem is soluble, every ill curable, every need answerable...In these first days of the '70s, there is an end to innocence."

> On every hand our technology seems either to fail us or burden us. Our power appears impotent in Asia. Our autos are increasingly paralyzed on our highways....Our telephones falter, our electric power repeatedly threatens to fail us. We agonize...that our schools don't educate, our culture doesn't civilize....
>
> From this mixture of expectation, of affluence, of technical mastery, of mushrooming growth...has emerged an increasing doubt about our purposes, individual and national. At the very peak of our progress, the air is foul, the beaches are filthy, the lakes and rivers die, some plants wither, birds flee, the garbage piles up.... If there is no certainty to be found in power, religion, wealth or science, then to many...all that seems to remain is oneself—one's appetites, needs, feelings, perceptions.[6]

Affluence itself, supposedly a cause for rejoicing, is often cited as a root cause of humanist dissatisfaction. The dehumanizing effects of substituting a machine for the labor of man has been

---

[3] Daniel Bell. "The Idea of a Social Report," *The Public Interest,* Spring 1969, p. 72.

[4] "The Mood of America Today," *U.S. News & World Report,* April 20, 1970.

[5] Howard K. Smith, "Frustrated America: Symptoms, Causes, and Cures," *The Humanist,* February 1970, p. 14.

[6] Leo Cherne, address before Business Publications Audit, Chicago, Feb. 18, 1970.

a familiar subject of social criticism since the beginning of the industrial revolution in 18th century England. But it can be argued that the dispossessed worker's sense of psychological deprivation is deeper today than ever because he is surrounded by an affluent society. Other members of that society seem to have passed him by. Moreover, it is a society in which individual craftsmanship is of diminishing importance.

Many social commentators say that speed of change in itself is disrupting the individual's sense of his own identity and alienating him from a society which seems to race ahead of him. To Alvin Toffler, author of *Future Shock,* the rapid pace of change is a central fact of our times, quite apart from the actual nature of the change. "A fire storm of change... spawns in its wake all sorts of curious flora—from psychedelic churches and 'free universities' to science cities in the Arctic and wife-swap clubs in California." Toffler defines future shock as a "new disease" caused by "the dizzying disorientation brought on by the premature arrival of the future."[7]

"There cannot be many sophisticated Americans who have not...had the sense that they are refugees of time and identity, if not of place," Peter Schrag writes. He speaks of "tensions of estrangement" due to "the events and the forces we have created, and which we honor but which tend to displace and destroy." War, the nuclear arms race, technology, "mass media homogenization," bureaucracy, and even public schools are all considered part of the alienating process. "The center in which Americans believed is beset by organizational and technological complexity; it becomes unmanageable and we all become displaced persons...."[8]

Above all other factors tending to create a sense that humane values are slipping away is the nature of modern weaponry, epitomized by nuclear arsenals. The creation of the first atomic bomb and its release over Hiroshima and Nagasaki 25 years ago constituted a kind of watershed in human experience. "From now onward," Arthur Koestler told the 14th Nobel Symposium in Stockholm in September 1969, "our species lives on borrowed time." "It carries a time bomb fastened round its neck. We shall have to listen to the sound of

---

[7] Alvin Toffler, *Future Shock* (1970), pp. 11-13.
[8] Peter Schrag, "Out of Place in America: Confessions of a Chauvinist," *Saturday Review,* May 9, 1970, p. 13. His article was taken from a new book of essays, *Out of Place in America.*

its ticking...for decades and centuries to come, until either it
blows up or we succeed in defusing it."[9]

Depersonalizing influences in modern life have led not only
to protest and social criticism but to numerous efforts to re-
store a sense of personal identity and community with other
people. The humanizing trend in religion, for example, puts
less emphasis on ritual and more on giving witness to Christian precepts in personal relations with others. This outlook is
manifest in many ways—anti-war and social protest activities
of clergymen, resistance of Catholic priests to the celibacy
rule, secularization of nuns' dress and the character of their
services in the community, opening of church doors to alienated youth, growing acceptance of change in the code of sexual
morals, and introduction of youth-culture music and dance in
religious celebrations.[10]

Efforts to Achieve Sense of Human Community

Much of the youth culture is a form of asserting personal
individuality or a seeking of closer contact with others in
what seems a hostile or indifferent world. This is especially
apparent in the music of youth, both in the music itself which
is often a bombardment of the senses and in the accompanying lyrics that express the longings, the resentments, the
hopes or the hopelessness of its special audience.

"The music is implicitly condemning the fragmentation
of the individual's life which is endemic in the modern world.
The songsters are saying that it is wrong to compartmentalize
work and play, wrong to cut men off from the natural rhythm
of nature, wrong to stifle sex and love and play in favor of
greater productivity, wrong to say man's spiritual needs can
be filled by providing him with more material possessions...."[11] For some young people who seek a more intense
realization of their internal world, this road led to drugs and
a cutoff from the world of external reality.

Communal living represents an attempt to achieve a greater
sense of fellowship with others than has seemed possible in

---

[9] See Arthur Koestler, "Man—One of Evolution's Mistakes?" *The New York Times
Magazine,* Oct. 19, 1969, and "Nuclear Balance of Terror: 25 Years After Alamogordo,"
E.R.R., 1970 Vol. II, pp. 483-504.

[10] See Eugene C. Bianichi's article, "John XXIII, Vatican II and American Catholicism," *Annals of the American Academy of Arts and Science,* January 1970, and "Religion in Upheaval," *E.R.R.,* 1967 Vol. II, pp. 1-20.

[11] Robert A. Rosenstone (associate professor, California Institute of Technology), "The
Music of Protest," *Annals of the American Academy of Arts and Science,* March 1969,
pp. 132-134.

conventional living. Communards in the wilderness seek, in addition, a personal fulfillment in natural surroundings. They shun comforts and conveniences for which, in their mind, civilization extracts too high a price. Hippies and cop-outs are not the only ones who take to the wilderness route. Many relatively conventional individuals are choosing to live on a more primitive level than they need to in places remote from metropolitan areas. The mobility of Americans can be attributed in part to a desire to escape from "our alienated, technological, and technopathic society"—the very society that provides the means for securing a "portable life-support system for a reasonable investment."[12]

The reach for more human contact takes many different forms. It was the main theme of the very beginning of student unrest in the 1960s. Students directed their protest at first against the impersonality of university bureaucracy and the remoteness of faculty members. This sense of protest was conveyed in the humanist message on buttons worn by students during the first of the major student demonstrations, at the University of California at Berkeley in 1964. The message was: "Do not fold, spindle or mutilate."

Still other evidence of the effort to overcome the impersonality that characterizes modern life is the encounter-group movement—or fad, as some view it. As described in the book *Please Touch* (1969) by Jane Howard, a young woman who participated in a number of encounter groups on a reportorial assignment:

> ...An encounter group is a gathering, for a few hours or a few days, of 12 or 18 personable, responsible, certifiably normal... people. Their destination is intimacy, trust and awareness of why they behave as they do in groups; their vehicle is candor. Exhorted to "get in touch with their feelings" and to "live in the here-and-now," they sprawl on the floor...[or] rest their heads on rolled-up sweaters [or] on each other's laps. In many instances they have never even met before, but, like the proverbial strangers on a train, quickly talk of their deepest emotions."

Encounter groups and other forms of "sensitivity training"—literally to sensitize the participants to the human qualities of each other—have attracted the interest of education officials, business executives and psychologists. A growing number of psychologists in America and abroad view them-

---

[12] "The New Gypsies," *Esquire*, September 1970, pp. 109-110. See "Communal Living," *E.R.R.*, 1969 Vol. II, pp. 575-594.

selves as "humanistic psychologists," a term that signifies their rejection of the two major movements in psychology in this century—psychoanalysis and behaviorism[13]—and their turn toward encounter-group techniques. Humanistic psychology has achieved formal status as a separate discipline. The American Association of Humanistic Psychology was founded in 1962 and its convention in Miami Beach, Fla., in September 1970 attracted about 1,500 psychologists, teachers, sociologists, students, and others. During the previous month, the first International Conference on Humanistic Psychology was held at Amsterdam.

Humanism and Western Civilization

THE HUMANIST SPIRIT in some form or degree has doubtless existed since the dawn of civilization. The first assertion of the humanist position may well have been that of Protagoras, Greek philosopher of the fifth century B.C., who said: "Man is the measure of all things." That is, man is the standard of what is true to himself; all truth is relative to the individual who holds it. Modern humanism descends, through many byways and with many branchings out, from the intellectual awakening in western Europe that began in the 14th century. Humanism arose first in Italy where the great city states, like the United States today, were enjoying a growth of affluence based on a booming commercial economy. "Only in a consumers' civilization...,founded on wealth and leisure, could such a movement take place."[14]

Renaissance Humanism and Its Greek Heritage

The humanism of the Renaissance was a literary and intellectual movement marked by enthusiasm for the study and imitation of the art and literature of ancient Greece and Rome. While study of the classics may seem a far cry from what

---

[13] Psychoanalysis, building on the insights and clinical experience of Sigmund Freud, is based on a search for childhood experience and unconscious motivation as roots of behavior; behaviorism starts with the act of response to stimulus and builds through the conditioning theory of B.F. Skinner to the picture of man's current behavior as a variation of past learning and exposure to social models. See James Moriarty's "A Third Force Arises in Psychology," *Science News*, Sept. 19, 1970, pp. 256-257.

[14] Edward P. Cheyney, "Humanism," *Encyclopedia of Social Sciences* (1937), Vol. IV, p. 537.

today's alarm-criers and reformists have in mind when they speak of humanism, in that earlier time the plunge into the all-but-forgotten pagan world of the distant past constituted a celebration of the rediscovery of man as a human creature. Poets, scholars, artists, copyists, and other enthusiasts for classic works found in them the inspiration for a new outlook on life. "Gradually the old classical conception of man as an autonomous, independent, rational human being began to be revived. That long-forgotten appreciation of the value and dignity of the human personality...so long buried under the weight of Christian humility and other-worldliness, now re-emerged."[15]

Will Durant has written that the "humanists captivated the mind of Italy, turned it from...heaven to earth, and revealed to an astonished generation the riches of pagan thought and art." "The proper study of mankind was now to be man, in all the joy and pain of his senses and feelings, in all the frail majesty of his reason." "The humanists," Durant added, "liberated man from dogma, taught him to love life rather than brood about death, and made the European mind free."[16]

Though its spirit was secular, humanism extended its sway to men of the church. Erasmus, the archetypal humanist in the Renaissance of the North, was an ordained priest who never renounced his vows, though he managed miraculously —considering the age he lived in—to maintain an extraordinary freedom of mind, utterance, and life style as a wandering scholar. Erasmus is often pictured as an early model of modern man, that is if one thinks of modern man in terms of the humanist ideal—urbane, tolerant, reasonable, open-minded, intellectually curious, appreciative and knowledgable in *belles lettres,* a moderate and man of good will who speaks not for a particular group but for all humanity.

"In spite of his extreme individualism, in spite of his being so profoundly a man of his time," a French authority on Erasmus wrote of the great humanist 400 years after his birth in Rotterdam, "...we cannot help recognizing in Erasmus a universal thinker...free from the temptations and snares of anti-humanistic nationalism, whether viewed in terms of his own 16th century or our 20th century." "He

---

[15] W. Y. Jones, *A History of Western Philosophy* (1953), p. 565.
[16] Will Durant, *The Story of Civilization: Part V, The Renaissance* (1953), pp. 77-78, 86.

The New Humanism

never abandoned his watchtower regard for the human person, reaffirming his resolve to stand halfway between two concepts: God is all, man is nothing and Man's freedom can conquer everything."[17] Erasmus' pacifism had a modern ring. He opposed the holy war between Christians and Turks, condemning barbarism and intolerance on both sides. "The majority of the people hate war," he wrote in *Complaint of Peace*. "A minority whose wretched good fortune always depends on the misery of the people, wants war. Must their inhumanity outweigh the will of so many good people?"

Influence of Enlightenment on Founding Fathers

Over the years, the term "humanism" has taken on new meanings, though a certain underlying theme remained constant: that "knowledge was...to proceed from and return to the glory and dignity of man."[18] A contemporary British humanist describes humanism as having "connotations of cultural width and of generosity of spirit...[implying] not only an intellectual interest in everything relating to humanity, but also a conviction that humanity is worth caring for."[19] Much of what is considered humanism today stems from the 18th century Enlightenment which sustained the humanist spirit in its elevation of free thought and reason as prime resources for creating the good life for man. It, too, was anti-theological and admiring of the classics.

Through the influence of the Enlightenment, the humanist ideal was implanted in the United States by the founding fathers. The evidence of this shows in many ways: the separation of church and state, the naming of the chief legislative body the "Senate," the revival of the Greek motif in federal architecture, and the classical curriculum of the early institutions of higher education. In the words of Howard Mumford Jones: "The young republic was nourished in the matrix of humanism, of that 18th century humanism which emphasized, not the virtue dear to the Renaissance, but reason dear to the Enlightenment."

Humanitarianism of the 19th century is sometimes linked to humanism, though the tone of the two movements differed. While both were concerned with man's temporal welfare, the humanitarian movement lacked the intellectual overtones

[17] Jean-Claude Margolin, "Erasmus: Universal Thinker of Yesterday for Today," *UNESCO Courier*, November 1969, pp. 5-12.
[18] Howard Mumford Jones, *American Humanism* (1957), p. 29
[19] Cyril Bibby, "The Scientific Humanist Culture," *The Humanist Outlook* (edited by A. J. Ayer, 1968), p. 13.

of humanism. It tended to emotionalism and sentimentality while humanism relied on reason. "Despite its humane spirit humanism struck at best merely a loose alliance with humanitarianism... Except for its early enthusiasm for the classics, humanism has not been characterized by intense emotion. Revolt against injustice, cruelty and unnecessary suffering or hardship was, to be sure, a mark of the humanistic spirit, and humanitarian reforms could count on a certain amount of sympathy from persons dominated by that spirit."[20]

Neo-Humanists as Twentieth-Century Reformists

In the present century, the term "new humanists" or "neo-humanists" has been applied to a group of writers, scholars and educators who developed a point of view critical of certain trends in American society that they deemed inimical to the humanist ideal. They were particularly critical of American education for having discarded the earlier goal of broadly educating individuals in favor of training mere workers for a technology-based society. Such criticism is still voiced by persons who call themselves humanists.

The American Humanist Association publishes many varieties of contemporary humanist thought and social criticism in its bi-monthly journal, *The Humanist.* The range of contemporary American humanist interests, as indicated by the journal, includes environmental questions, conscription and conscientious objection, abortion reform, sexual morality, and the impact of technology on man and society. The journal's tone is reformist but not doctrinaire.[21] Articles are never exhortatory; humanists favor "dialogues" and forums. Humanists are not soap-box orators and they are rarely called on, or seek to be called on, to testify as humanists before legislative committees or other investigative bodies on specific issues. They seek a more pervasive influence on the way thinking Americans think.

Nevertheless this relatively bland, loosely allied grouping of highly educated Americans, as much given to self-criticism as to criticizing other elements of modern society, has often been subjected to attack and these attacks at times have been sufficient to ruffle the equanimity of spokesmen for

---

[20] Cheney, *op. cit.*, p. 541.

[21] *The Humanist* describes itself as "a journal of contemporary ethical concern that attempts to serve as a bridge between theoretical philosophical discussions and the practical applications of humanism to ethical and social problems and the lives of individuals."

the humanist way of life. An editor of *The Humanist*, for example, found it necessary to answer the charge that the publication condoned the permissive society. "To advocate a society free of obsolete moral restrictions does not mean that one is arguing for the absence of all rules," the editor wrote.

> It is simply to say that the rules we develop should be appropriate to the needs and experiences of people, and...should not be imposed...by arbitrary authority....Instead of...the permissive society, we ought perhaps to speak of the *civilized* society—for that is what we really want. A society in which I will tolerate your rights on the condition that you tolerate and respect mine.[22]

"The AHA is not for everyone," the association states in a bid for membership. "It serves best those who choose to help shape their own destiny, who wish to have a constructive philosophy...who wish for action to be more than emotional responses to situations, and to help reconstruct both the social scene and individual lives."

'Secular Religion' of Humanism Versus the Church

Humanism is sometimes attacked as a specious effort to establish a secular religion. An advisory committee to the California State Department of Education issued a report in 1969 that attacked modern humanism as an "atheist creed" infecting the schools. The report, *Guidelines for Moral Instruction in California Schools,* linked humanism with a breakdown in moral standards and with pressure for sex education. It noted that John Dewey, "known commonly as the high priest of 'progressive education'," was one of the signers of *A Humanist Manifesto,* published in 1933.

On another level of criticism, the alleged pretensions of humanism as a substitute for religion were condemned in the liberal weekly *The Nation,* in an article by Ronald Sampson, lecturer in politics and author of *The Psychology of Power* (1966). Sampson objected to the humanist position that man can seek good by exercise of reason, without invoking belief in a deity. Doing good offers no inducement, he argued,unless it is in obedience to a higher authority. For instance, to stop warfare requires a degree of trust so dangerous to individual and group survival that one would have to believe that God wills it before embarking on such a course.[23]

---

[22] "Notes From the Editor," *The Humanist,* November-December 1969.
[23] Ronald Sampson, "The Vanity of Humanism," *The Nation,* Dec. 29, 1969, pp. 718-725.

Humanism and religious piety are by no means incompatible. There are Christian humanists as there are atheist and agnostic humanists. Humanism has obviously had considerable impact on religious practice. There were humanist elements in the social action movement of the churches earlier in this century and there are even more in the recent efforts to bring the churches "into the street." A leading expression of this trend was voiced in the best-seller of several years ago, *The Secular City* (1965), by Harvey Cox, an ordained Baptist minister.

Catholicism was strongly opposed to modern humanism until two or three decades ago. The French anthropologist-priest, Pierre Teilhard de Chardin, is credited with having welded elements of the humanist outlook with Catholic theology. His most popular book, *The Phenomenon of Man,* first published in translation in the United States in 1960, viewed the evolution of man as a process leading through natural phenomena to his elevation as a moral and religious person. A Jesuit professor of philosophy at Fordham University has written: "Teilhard's appeal came from the fact that for the first time in recent history a Catholic spokesman was trying to show that concern for the things of this world can be important for religious development."[24] Vatican Council II, held October 1962-December 1965, helped open the door to a more humanist outlook within the church. Though Catholic thinking still tends to be cautious, there seems to be less suspicion of humanism than in the past.

Science on Defensive Against Humanist Criticism

Humanism has jousted with science as well as with religion. Though humanism has always been devoted to free inquiry and the exercise of man's reason—two hallmarks of scientific endeavor—the discoveries of scientists since the 17th century have tended to reduce man's stature in the natural scheme of things and this was not a palatable concept to the true humanist. A body of thought known as naturalism, which viewed man as simply one phenomenon among many in the natural order of things, was opposed to the humanist view.

Science proved troublesome in other ways, too. The practical applications of scientific discoveries in the 19th century put a pragmatic stamp on education which bothers humanists to

---

[24] Robert S. Roth, "Humanism and Catholicism," *The Humanist,* September-October 1969, pp. 28-30.

this day. The old idea of science as a part of philosophy and hence a proper subject for nurturing the humanist mind was supplanted by the introduction of practical science. As late as 1957 a modern humanist, Howard Mumford Jones, complained that American humanism had been reduced to a mere collection of subjects labeled "humanities" which took second place to science and the so-called social sciences.

Insofar as technological advance is a product of scientific discovery, this old conflict between science and humanism has taken a critical turn. The marshalling of scientific brains during World War II to produce the atomic bomb was a blow to the concept of science as a source of continuing benefit to man. The drawbacks of science then became apparent.

"It is incredible, but true, that science and its technologies are today on the defensive," the director of the Oak Ridge (Tenn.) National Laboratory said in an address to fellow scientists abroad. The assault was coming from "muckrakers, mostly journalists, who picture the scientific enterprise as being corrupted by political maneuvering for the scientific dollar"; from officials who feel science has little to say about grave social questions of the day; from "technological critics who urge a slowdown...because of its detrimental side effects"; and from "scientific abolitionists: the very noisy, usually young, critics who consider the whole scientific-technological, if not rationalistic, mode of the past 100 years a catastrophe."[25]

The scientific community has indicated some responsiveness to criticism along humanist lines. The American Association for the Advancement of Science agreed at a board meeting in October 1969 that for the coming decade the main thrust of its attention and resources "shall be dedicated to a major increase in work on the chief contemporary problems concerning the relations of science, technology and social change, including the uses of science and technology in the promotion of human welfare." Various scientific meetings held under association auspices showed that "the center of concern is shifting...from too much emphasis on specialized matters...toward problems affecting all of science, all scientists, and the society in which they function."[26]

---

[25] Alvin M. Weinberg, "In Defense of Science," *Science,* Jan. 9, 1970, p. 141. The article was adapted from the author's address, Oct. 18, 1969, to the Association of German Scientists at Munich.

[26] W. G. Berl, "The 1969 Meeting of the AAAS: A Brief Appraisal," *Science,* Feb. 20, 1970, p. 1158.

Meanwhile, self-doubt has entered the ranks of that small band who consider themselves custodians of the humanist tradition. Elements of the humanist position that had been considered most secure—represented by the terms "liberal," "reasonable," "sane," "constructive," "tolerant"—became suspect, challenged by the best students. A professor of English history has been moved to ask: Were humanists of his stamp being phased out? Should they place their "humanist assumptions in escrow?"[27]

New Challenges to Humanist Ideals

THE HUMANIST OUTLOOK produces both optimists and pessimists. Arnold Toynbee, the British historian, can be counted among the pessimists. He finds a "persistent vein of violence and cruelty in human nature" and wonders whether the achievements of Western civilization are going to survive. "What is the lesson of our unforeseen and disillusioning experience?" he asks. "It has taught us that, though progress may be cumulative in the fields of science and technology, there is no such thing as cumulative progress towards an ever-greater humanity in our treatment of each other."—"We realize now that Hitlerism was not just an isolated aberration."[28]

Albert Speer, a surviving architect of Nazism, projects the theme of technology and humanism a step further. In his recently published memoirs, *Inside the Third Reich* (1970), Speer quotes from his final speech as a contrite defendant at the Nuremberg war crimes trials. "Every country in the world today faces the danger of being terrorized by technology," he said, "but in a modern dictatorship this seems to me to be unavoidable." "Therefore, the more technological the world becomes, the more essential will be the demand for individual freedom and the self-awareness of the individual human being as a counterpoise to technology."

Zbigniew Brzezinski is among the scholars who believe the doom-sayers do not fully recognize the potential of technolo-

---

[27] R. J. Kaufmann, "On Knowing One's Place: A Humanistic Meditation," *Daedalus,* Summer 1969, pp. 699-713.

[28] Arnold Toynbee, writing in *Los Angeles Times,* Sept. 6, 1970.

gy for attaining humanist goals. In his new book, *Between Two Ages* (1970), he attributes the trials of the present to the pangs of transition from the industrial to the "technetronic" (technology-electronics) era of the future—a change which he expects to be as momentous for man as the transition from the agrarian to the industrial age. Technetronics will free man from the "grubby, daily struggle against his environment" and give him time to ponder his place in the universe. Brzezinski contends that some steps toward that freedom have already been taken. "For the first time we are able to inquire 'To what end? What purpose should society serve? What am I, who am I, what am I for?' "[29]

R. Buckminster Fuller, a technologist who was chosen "Humanist of the Year" in 1969 by the American Humanist Association, takes an optimistic view of man's potential state. "I find very unsympathetic and short-sighted statements being made about technology...as something very independent of man," he said in his acceptance address. "I do not see technology as something...foreign to man....I am convinced that whatever nature permits is natural...[and nature] has in it the option that man can employ to alter the environment to the advantage of his fellow man." Fuller believes that computers and other instruments of automation can save man from the curse of over-specialization and force him "back to his innate comprehensivist role—to be really the humanist."

Fate of Humane Values in Fast-Changing Times

Changing physical conditions of life—affluence, crowding in cities, rapid communications, new weaponry, the pill—have already affected the general acceptance of certain values once considered eternal. Emmanuel G. Mesthene, director of the Harvard University Program on Technology and Society, has pointed out that the advance of technology requires planning, and planning requires value judgments in establishing priorities. It is this that pushes conflict to the fore. "The increased awareness of conflicts among our values that planning and rational decision-making produce serves in part to explain the generally questioning attitude toward traditional values that appears to be endemic to a high-technology, knowledge-based society."[30]

---

[29]Quoted in *The New York Times*, Aug. 12, 1970. Brzezinski is professor of government at Columbia University and a former member of the State Department's Policy Planning Council (1966-68).

[30] Emmanuel G. Mesthene, *Technological Change: Its Impact on Man and Society* (1970), p. 46.

One reason technology has a direct impact on values, he added, is that it increases the number of available options. Or it may change their relative costs as to favor one or another choice. For example, computer technology now used for rapid collection of voter opinion might eventually provide for "instant voting" by the entire electorate only hours after a President presented an issue over television. "It thus raises the possibility of instituting a genuine system of direct democracy," Mesthene said. This might appeal to those who advocate more popular participation in the political process but it "arouses the apprehension of those...who treasure the potentials for public education and sober political judgment implicit in our existing system."

Another question concerns the fate of the values implied in the term "work ethic." If technology plus affluence should markedly reduce the hours of human labor required to produce enough for all, what happens to the values associated with work-for-pay? There are serious thinkers today who suspect that the wandering youths who live by begging, pilfering, or remittances from relatives may be precursors of a life style to be widely adopted in the future. The meaning of life then may derive from other kinds of activity than paid employment. Leo Cherne, looking ahead to the year 2000, has said he expects more young people to drop out. "We will not only tolerate their dropping out, we will finally be content to subsidize them."

Biological Controls Over Nature of Future Man

Perhaps the most important choice that will have to be made is the kind of human being that man is to become. Technological advance can change not only the environment of man and the way in which he spends his days but eventually it may also change man himself. The following is by no means a solitary vision of the possibility of such change:

> Humanity today is on the threshold of self-transfiguration, of attaining new powers over itself and its environment that can alter its nature as fundamentally as walking upright or the use of tools. No aspect of man's existence can escape being revolutionized by this fundamental fact—all his self-consciousness that we call culture, his patterns of interaction that we call society, his very biological structure itself....Man is still capable of fundamental change ...evolution has not come to an end.[31]

---

[31] Victor C. Ferkiss, *Technological Man* (1969), pp. 18-19.

Biological science, with its prospects for "genetic engineering," forces a reappraisal of such age-old verities as the distinction between life and death, the nature of man, the autonomy of the individual person, and the quality of human freedom. The Center for the Study of Democratic Institutions at Santa Barbara, Calif., held a conference in 1969 on the social and ethical implications of the "biological revolution." Among the present and prospective biological advances discussed at the conference were these:

A process called "cloning" that makes it possible to replicate the genetic characteristics of an organism by starting with the cells of a single parent organism. This has already been accomplished with rats and chickens; according to Robert L. Sinsheimer, chairman of the division of biology at California Institute of Technology, it could become possible in human organisms within 10 to 20 years.

Control of the sex of the newborn, also a possibility within 10 to 20 years.

Potential ability to alter inherited physiological or psychological processes.

Prolongation of human life through organ transplant or regeneration.

Control through genetic manipulation of human instincts, drives and emotions.

"To what extent can man retain his humanity in the new brave world of technological science and biological transmutation?" one of the participating scientists asked.[32] Such manipulation can of course be directed to either benign or malign purposes. Brainwashing techniques are no longer a novelty. How far they can go is a question. "I believe that the day has come when we can combine sensory deprivation with drugs, hypnosis and astute manipulation of reward and punishment to gain almost absolute control over an individual's behavior," wrote James V. McConnell, psychologist of the University of Michigan. "It should be possible then to...make dramatic changes in a person's behavior and personality." He saw this as a potential means of crime control. "I foresee the day when we could convert the worst criminal into a decent respectable citizen in a matter of a few months—or perhaps even less time." There was a catch, or course. "We could also do the opposite...change a decent respectable citizen into a criminal."[33]

---

[32] Kurt Reinhardt, professor emeritus at Stanford University, quoted in *The Center Magazine*, November 1969, p. 34.

[33] James V. McConnell, "Criminals Can Be Brainwashed—Now," *Psychology Today*, April 1970, p. 14.

Some of the hazards of eliminating destructive drives in man were indicated by Konrad Lorenz, who is called the founding father of ethology, the study of animal behavior. If aggression in man were somehow removed to eliminate war and crime, there might also be a loss of impetus for tackling tasks or problems affecting everything "from the morning shave to the sublimest artistic or scientific creations." Man might even lose that "very important and specifically human faculty [of]...laughter."[34]

In a recent interview, Lorenz expressed a fear commonly heard on the subject of conditioning men to attain social goals: "that the 'Establishment', as it exists in either the West or the East, will undertake a selection of conformists...."[35] Even if technology should provide the means to make everyone content, it is doubtful that man would ever be ready to pay the price of submission—the loss of some measure of his own humanity.

---

[34] Konrad Lorenz, *On Aggression* (1963), p. 278.
[35] "A Talk With Konrad Lorenz," *The New York Times Magazine*, July 5, 1970, p. 29.

URBANIZATION OF THE EARTH

by

Richard C. Schroeder

**1 9 7 0
May 20**

URBANIZATION OF THE EARTH

THROUGHOUT THE WORLD cities and towns are growing at a pace that far outstrips the population increase of the countryside. Rapid and widespread urbanization adds another dimension to man's already serious population problem. The issue is not merely one of numbers, but of distribution. Excessive crowding brings a multitude of urban ills—air and water pollution, traffic jams, housing shortages and crime. Perhaps worst of all is the apparent inability of governments to deal with such problems.

It can be argued that the major crises facing man, from environmental pollution to crime and violence to poverty, are all related in some way to the groundswell of urbanization. Paradoxically, as human society becomes more and more urbanized, the cities themselves deteriorate at an alarming rate. The "inner cities" and downtown areas of some of the world's principal urban agglomerations are decaying shells, becoming increasingly unfit for human habitation. In city after city, the downtown area is losing population to the burgeoning suburbs. To some observers, "the age of the city seems to be at an end"[1] at the very moment urbanization of the earth is at hand.

Rapid urbanization is not confined to the United States, nor even to industrialized countries. "Before 1850 no society could be described as predominantly urbanized, and by 1900 only one—Great Britain—could be so regarded. Today, all industrial nations are highly urbanized, and in the world as a whole the process of urbanization is accelerating rapidly.... Clearly the world as a whole is not fully urbanized, but it soon will be."[2] In the past decade, Middle America (Central America and Mexico) and Tropical South America became predominantly urban. Demographers now class all of the Western Hemisphere urban—50 per cent or more of the people live in

---

[1] Melvin M. Webber, "The Post-City Age," *Daedalus*, Fall 1968. Webber notes that "The phrase is Don Martindale's." It closes Martindale's introduction to Max Weber's *The City* (1962)

[2] Kingsley Davis, "The Urbanization of the Human Population," *Cities* (1966), p. 4.

urban areas—except the underdeveloped islands of the Caribbean.

The 1970 census of the Soviet Union showed that for the first time a majority of its population was urban. Cities accounted for 136 million, 56 per cent of the nation's people, in contrast to 100 million and 48 per cent in 1959. Soviet policy is intended to hold back the growth of large cities but Moscow officials, even with the aid of central planning, were unable to keep the capital from reaching a population of seven million, two million more than was intended. Whereas only three Russian cities exceeded the million mark in 1959, ten did in 1970. In the United States, three-quarters of the population is classified as urban, in contrast to one-fifth a century ago. Britain, which began the urban transformation before any other country, is more than 80 per cent urbanized.

The definition of "urban" varies from country to country. A nation with big rural villages that are almost exclusively agricultural may not classify a settlement as urban until it reaches 5,000 inhabitants. Another country, with many small towns that are more industrial than agricultural, may set the rural limit at 2,000. In the United States, the Census Bureau classifies any settlement bigger than 2,500 as urban. The bureau defines a "city" as having at least 100,000 persons and an "urbanized area" as one or more central cities of 50,000, together with closely surrounding areas. A metropolitan area—officially a "Standard Metropolitan Statistical Area"—is the central city and the surrounding counties. [3]

As defined by the United Nations, the urban population of the world—all localities with 20,000 inhabitants or more—rose from 253 million in 1920 to 753 million in 1960. The bulk of this growth took place in underdeveloped countries, those least equipped to handle it. "In the less developed regions, the urban population has increased fourfold in the past forty years," a United Nations official said in 1970. "In the year 2000 it may be twenty times as large as it was in the year 1920." [4] By the end of the 1970s some 18 cities in Latin America

---

[3] The difference between an urbanized area and a metropolitan area is usually very small. The population of American cities given in this report includes the surrounding areas, unless otherwise noted.

[4] Eric Carlson (chief of housing section of United Nations Centre for Housing, Building and Planning), in speech before United Nations Seminar on Improvement of Slums and Uncontrolled Settlements, Medellin, Colombia—quoted in *Survey of Economic Development* (publication of Society for International Development), April 1970, p. 3. Other U.N. population figures cited are derived from the United Nations publication *Urbanization: Development Policies* (1968).

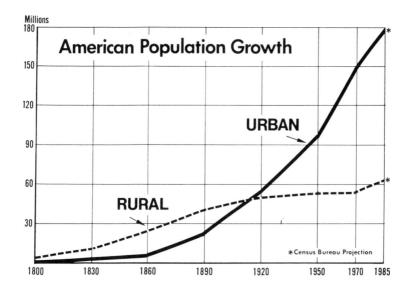

Millions

American Population Growth

URBAN

RURAL

*Census Bureau Projection

1800 1830 1860 1890 1920 1950 1970 1985

will each have exceeded one million population. Two of these will be in Colombia, where government publicists are already calling the country "a land of cities." Latin America's biggest city, Buenos Aires, is expected to reach 12 million by the end of the decade. In India, Calcutta will probably almost equal the present population of the sprawling New York-New Jersey metropolitan area (see table, page 27). If present trends continue throughout the decade, the urban population of developing countries will outnumber city dwellers of advanced countries by 100 million.

City as Prime Cause and Victim of Pollution

All human activity tends to pollute the earth and atmosphere; where human activity is greater then so is pollution. Thus the city is a prime cause—and victim—of pollution. Cities and industries along the shores of Lake Erie have turned it into a "dead sea" with their outpouring of wastes. Astronaut Wally Schirra reported from his Apollo 7 space flight that he was unable to see much of California—it was hidden beneath a shroud of smog. Dr. John T. Middleton, director of the National Air Pollution Control Administration, views pollution as one of the most serious problems that man has ever faced.

A recent scientific analysis of New York City's atmosphere indicated that a New Yorker on the street took into his lungs the equivalent in toxic materials of 38 cigarettes a day. Noting that analysis, two authors wrote: "Suddenly all the scientific jargon, official warnings, reams of statistics—the overwhelming avalanche of damning facts concerning America's air pollution—took focus. Here was a reduction of the tons of soot, sulphides, monoxide, hydrocarbons, etc., into simple, understandable personal terms."

> These figures are of vital interest to two-thirds of the population, which is the percentage of Americans who already live in 212 standard metropolitan areas having only 9 per cent of the nation's land area but 99 per cent of its pollution. Some cities outdo Manhattan and on days of cloud and atmospheric inversion actually kill off small segments of their excess population.... [5]

Scientists now confirm that cities are hotter and smellier than the countryside. A recent study showed that the air temperature in Columbia, a new town near Washington, D.C., was 10 degrees higher than in fields and forests, and that air pollutants, notably sulphur dioxide, were 10 per cent more numerous. The chief culprit in urban pollution is the internal combustion engine, although any kind of burning obviously adds pollutants, and heat, to the urban atmosphere. [6]

Pollution is a problem not only in the United States. Cities throughout the world are fighting, and generally losing, a battle against smog, filthy rivers and mounting piles of solid wastes. Intensive anti-pollution campaigns in Britain have alleviated the smog problem in London but not in the industrial Midlands. The River Plate, draining a rich basin that includes parts of Argentina, Bolivia, Paraguay, Brazil and Uruguay, has been called "the dirtiest river in the world." The famed bathing beaches of Argentina and Uruguay along its shores are in danger of being closed. One tributary of the River Plate, the Riachuelo, literally runs black with filth as it flows through the heart of the Buenos Aires industrial district. Natives of Buenos Aires call it "la cloaca," the sewer.

The Council of Europe convoked a meeting of 24 nations in February 1970 to consider environmental problems stemming from "urban conglomeration" and industrialization. The meeting cited "special dangers" from the rush of building along the shores of the Mediterranean, in Scandinavia and along the Swiss lakes. The United States, too, has begun to awaken to the horrors of the urban environment. Environment may become the political issue of the decade. On Jan. 1, 1970, Presi-

---

[5] Robert Rienow and Leona Train Rienow, *Moment in the Sun* (1967), p. 141.

[6] See *The Environment Handbook*, edited by Garret de Bell (1970), prepared especially for the First Annual Environmental Teach-in, April 22, 1970.

LARGEST CITIES* OF THE WORLD

(Population in thousands)

City	1950	1960	1970
New York	12,331	14,114	16,077
Tokyo	6,277	9,684	12,119
London	10,393	10,953	11,544
Los Angeles	4,009	6,489	9,473
Buenos Aires	5,213	7,000	9,400
Paris	5,998	7,287	8,714
Shanghai	5,300	7,200	8,500
Sao Paulo	2,449	4,537	8,405
Peking	2,150	5,500	8,000
Calcutta	5,153	6,138	7,350
Rio de Janeiro	3,052	4,692	7,213
Chicago	4,935	5,959	6,983
Essen-Dortmund-Duisburg	4,597	5,587	6,789
Moscow	5,522	6,099	7,000
Cairo	2,502	3,747	5,600
Bombay	3,335	4,089	5,100
Seoul	1,467	2,445	4,661
Tientsin	2,200	3,500	4,500
Djakarta	1,452	2,852	4,500
San Francisco-Oakland	2,028	2,431	4,490
Detroit	2,667	3,538	4,447
Philadelphia	2,930	3,635	4,355
Wu-han	1,200	2,500	4,250
Hong Kong	1,561	3,075	4,105
Manila	1,781	2,704	4,100

*All population figures include metropolitan areas, except for Seoul, Tientsin and Djakarta.

SOURCES: *World Urbanization*, 1965-70, Vol. I *(Basic Data for Cities, Countries and Regions)*, et. al.

---

dent Nixon signed a bill creating a Council on Environmental Quality, and a month later he sent a pollution control message to Congress. Aware of the impact of the pollution issue on the electorate, Congress has appropriated $800 million for water pollution control in fiscal year 1970, four times the amount of two years earlier. The sum needed to clean up the air and water is reckoned in tens of billions.

Human and Financial Ills From Overcrowding

Noise is still another form of pollution, which scientists have begun to study only recently. Research so far indicates that the noises of a city—from aircraft, buses, subways, jackhammers—can raise the blood pressure, increase the cholesterol level, affect the heart and glands, harm unborn children, and cause stress and irritability. Perhaps even more alarming than the effects of noise is the discovery that crowding, itself, can contribute to neurosis, tumors, diseases of the vital organs and, in the extreme, death. Experiments with animals show that overcrowding produces abnormal physical and mental responses—a condition sometimes described as a "behavioral sink."

Dr. John B. Calhoun, a research psychologist at the National Institute of Mental Health, found that rats and mice subjected to overcrowding in a laboratory were driven to homosexuality, cannibalism and extreme withdrawal amounting to a denial of life. "He believes that not only is the parallel between human beings and his rodents about to come true all around our planet but that some of the effects are already visible in our crowded ghettos." [7] Some scientists attribute the high rate of violence and crime in cities to something akin to the "behavioral sink" in human affairs.

Among the many problems of cities, disposal of solid waste ranks high. Each year the average American throws away some 600 pounds of packaging material, much of it virtually indestructible. Solid wastes from the nation's urban areas are estimated to total 185 million tons a year. Cities spend $3 billion a year to rid themselves of their garbage, but that amount is not nearly enough. [8] Landfill for dumping near big cities is exceedingly scarce. Chicago has shipped the "sludge" residue from its sewage treatment plants to Florida by rail for use as fertilizer on citrus groves. Philadelphia has coveted abandoned mines hundreds of miles away. City dwellers even have difficulty finding sites for new cemeteries.

The housing shortage in many of the world's major cities is almost beyond the scope of human imagination. Shacks and shanty towns seem to be permanent features of any big city in a developing area. "Nearly every country has its own name for them. In Rio de Janeiro, they are 'favelas;' in Colombia, 'tugurios;' in Chile, 'callampas,' or mushroom towns. Whatever their names...slums are a way of life for millions." [9] Latin America needs one million units of new housing a year but only 400,000 are being built. According to projections cited by Galo Plaza, Secretary General of the Organization of

---

[7] Frank Sartwell, "The Small Satanic World of John B. Calhoun," *Smithsonian Magazine*, April 1970, p. 60.

[8] See "Waste Disposal: Coming Crisis," *E.R.R.*, 1969 Vol. I, pp. 185-201.

[9] Alliance for Progress *Weekly Newsletter*, July 26, 1965.

American States, the need will be more than two and a half times as great in 1975. In the affluent United States, the housing deficit amounts to 2.6 million units and has been described by George Romney, Secretary of Housing and Urban Development, as the worst since World War II. [10] Paradoxically, slum housing is being abandoned and left vacant at an increasing rate in big cities across the United States, either by tenants in fear of crime or by landlords as a bad investment.

Breakdown of Governmental Authority in Cities

From Rome to San Paulo, city dwellers tell horror stories of nonexistent services, monumental traffic snarls, communications breakdowns and of bureaucratic ineptitude in dealing with them. "All the big cities of mankind are sliding into chaos," according to Constantine Doxiadis, the city planning theorist. Wolf von Eckardt, urban affairs critic of *The Washington Post*, uses the term "urbicide" to describe what is happening to the major cities.

Governments demonstrate an inability to cope with problems in dozens of areas. Take transportation—the capital of the world's richest country has no rapid transit system. Construction of a Washington subway began in late 1969, after years of delay, but has been threatened with further delay by renewed bickering in Congress over District of Columbia affairs. Yet Washington's transportation problems are no worse than those of Rio de Janeiro, as anyone who has attempted the rush-hour trip from downtown Rio to Copacabana can attest. Communications networks are overloaded in all major cities. Breakdowns in telephone service are frequent even in the communications hub of the world, New York City. Power shortages have hit scores of urban areas across the nation since 1965, [11] and the President's chief science adviser, Dr. Lee A. DuBridge, has warned that more are likely in the summer of 1970.

Rising crime rates, terrorist bombings, public employee strikes, poor schools, race polarization—all these problems are identified largely with the urban community. In the long run, no problem is likely to prove more basic and less amenable to solution than unemployment. The supply of jobs in the cities—particularly in the developing world—is woefully inadequate for the huge and growing labor force. A recent estimate by the Inter-American Development Bank indicates that

---

[10] See "Private Housing Squeeze," *E.R.R.*, 1969 Vol. II, pp. 513-530.
[11] See "Electric Power Problems," *E.R.R.*, 1969 Vol. II, pp. 939-956.

30 per cent of the Latin American labor force may be unemployed or underemployed. In India, national planners estimate that 19 million new jobs will be created during the nation's fourth Five Year Plan (1966-71) but that 23 million workers will try to enter the labor force. Ten million Indians, officially, are already out of work. [12]

"Nor is there much evidence of any automatic corrective to today's broken rhythms of urban change," economist Barbara Ward said. "So long as cities are regarded as a byproduct of the total action of economic and social forces in a society and so long as these forces are essentially out of balance—too many people, too few jobs, too little capital, too much unskilled labor, stagnant farming, high-cost industry, small markets, big technologies—the cities are bound to become the areas where all the contradictions meet, clash and finally explode."

Calcutta as Archetype of Chaotic Urbanization

All the maladies of the Indian subcontinent seem concentrated in the teeming *bustees,* or slums, of Calcutta. Rudyard Kipling called Calcutta "the city of dreadful night." Others have labeled it "the city of death" and the "slum of the world," explaining that it is a "metropolis before its time." To anyone who has ever threaded his way over and around the hundreds of thousands of pitiful souls who sleep on the sidewalks of the city each night, Calcutta is the archetype of the world's urban chaos—a warning to all other cities of where the urban crisis may be leading them.

Calcutta is the world's tenth largest city, with a population in excess of seven million. It is the greatest port of India; its banks process 30 per cent of the country's banking transactions; its great jute mills are a mainstay of the Indian economy. And yet, "the city possesses no more than the rudiments of the technological apparatus that makes life possible for the comparable population and population density of London or New York...." [13]

More than three-fourths of the population of the city of Calcutta proper live in overcrowded tenement and *bustee*—slum—quarters. According to an official estimate, more than one-half of the *bustee* families live in cramped one-room quarters. One study showed that as many as 30 persons might share a single water tap and more than 20 a single latrine.

---

[12] Figures cited by Barbara Ward, "The Poor World's Cities," *The Economist,* Dec. 6, 1969.

[13] Nirmal Kumar Bose, "Calcutta: A Premature Metropolis," *Cities* (1966), pp. 60-61.

Calcutta is one of the cities of the underdeveloped world which grew up "out of phase with history," without the industrial jobs and social services which characterize the modern metropolis. Before the partition of India in 1947, Calcutta was already in desperate condition. Then, an influx of refugees from East Pakistan, brought on by communal strife between Hindus and Muslims, dealt Calcutta a blow from which it has never recovered. Estimates place the refugee population—most of it jobless, roofless and destitute—at more than one million. According to the chief engineer of the Calcutta Corporation, the city "was never planned."—"The city has grown up without anyone's ever expecting it to have any future." [14]

One-half of the city is without sewers, and there human waste collects in open ditches. The stench of Calcutta is never forgotten. Cholera is endemic and smallpox, malaria, tuberculosis and leprosy are prevalent. As many as 300,000 lepers live in Calcutta. More than 50 per cent of its people are illiterate and unemployment is chronic from the lowest levels of street sweepers through graduates of Calcutta University, the largest in the world. A single civil service opening attracts 4,000 applicants, *Newsweek* reported April 6, 1970.

In such circumstances, violence and civic rage are commonplace, erupting at the slightest provocation. Mobs have bombed buildings and burned autos over an issue no greater than a one-half-cent increase in streetcar fares. The ferocity of the mobs is matched only by the police who charge into them, swinging thick poles up to six feet in length, cracking skulls and smashing bones.

Changing Patterns of Metropolitan Growth

THE FIRST CITIES arose more than 5,000 years ago, in the so-called fertile crescent which covers much of the present Middle East. Compared with the metropolitan giants of today, the early cities were scarcely more than small towns. The population of Ur, one of the first Sumerian cities, is reckoned at a maximum of 34,000, and some authorities place it as low as 5,000. Within a few centuries of the appearance of Ur, rudi-

[14] Quoted by Ved Mehta, "City of Dreadful Night," *New Yorker*, March 21, 1970, p. 65.

mentary cities began to develop in the delta of the Nile River, and in the Indus Valley of modern Pakistan. [15] Less than a thousand years later, the first Chinese cities evolved in the middle reaches of the Yellow River. In the New World, urban settlements began to develop in the Mayan, Zapotecan, Mixtecan and, later, Aztecan cultures. The greatest of these, Teotihuacan, on the site of Mexico City, may have reached a population of 100,000 in the first millenium A.D.

Cities grew in response to a need for specialization of labor supplied by non-farm artisans. Most authorities agree that cities rose only after farming had advanced to a level where it could provide surpluses. They cite the late British archaeologist, V. Gordon Childe, who coined the phrase "urban revolution" and argued that an agricultural revolution preceded the urban revolution. Jane Jacobs disagrees, however. [16] The argument is of more than academic interest since it lies at the heart of problems of cities in underdeveloped countries. Barbara Ward lays heavy stress on agriculture as the basis for sound urbanization of those countries.

However cities came into being, they were spread over a large area of the known world by the Greek and Roman empires. When the Roman Empire broke up, the cities of Europe disappeared or shrank to small villages and towns. In 1600, only 1.6 per cent of the population of Europe lived in settlements of 100,000 or more; by 1800, only 2.2 per cent did. The industrial revolution changed all that, transforming first England and then much of northern Europe and the United States into predominantly urban societies. The modern metropolis is an industrial city, founded on manufacturing and allied industry. Its attractiveness lies in the availability of industrial employment.

City Migration Arising From Rural Stagnation

In the developing countries today, there is little connection between economic expansion and the explosive growth of cities. Urbanization in this case is based on agricultural stagnation. As a result, cities are expanding much faster than the economy. Unemployment is widespread, and governments—on the verge

---

[15] Gideon Sjoberg, "The Origin and Evolution of Cities," *Cities,* p. 28. See also Lewis Mumford, *The City in History* (1961).

[16] In her book *The Economy of Cities* (1969), Jane Jacobs wrote: "Current theory in many fields—economic, history, anthropology—assumes that cities are built on a rural economic base. If my observations and reasoning are correct, the reverse is true: that is, rural economies, including agricultural work, are directly built upon city economies and city work."

of bankruptcy—find it impossible to provide services essential to a growing population.

Migration from the countryside is an important part of the urbanization process in developing nations, but its importance is sometimes overstated. The principal factor in urban growth is the over-all population increase. World population growth averages 2 per cent a year—twice as fast as before World War II. In Latin America, the rate is almost 3 per cent. At that pace, its population of 280 million will double in less than a quarter of a century. Africa and Asia are only slightly behind. Cities on those three continents are growing 5 to 7 per cent a year and some are doubling their populations each decade. [17]

Urbanization is not necessarily the same as city growth. In a developed country such as the United States, three persons of every four already live in urban areas. Not much increase in the proportion of urban population can be expected. But the cities continue to grow, as the population continues to increase. Of the 100 million additional Americans expected by the end of this century, it is likely that 80 million will be city dwellers. [18]

No one is quite sure how the United States—or any other country—is going to accommodate the increase. The National Commission on Urban Problems recommended in 1969 that the nation, by the end of this century, build 100 new cities with 100,000 people each, and 10 with one million people each. More predictable than that, however, is the trend toward the "megalopolis," an urban complex embracing several core cities and their overlapping, sprawling suburbs. [19] Demographers identify at least three such complexes developing in the United States: "Boswash," the highly urbanized coastal strip between Boston and Washington, containing five of the 15 largest cities in the United States and upward of 40 million people; "Chipitts," the industrial stretch along the Great Lakes between Chicago and Pittsburgh; and "Sansan," between San Diego and San Francisco, embracing the Los Angeles-Long Beach urbanized area, the country's second largest. Similar megalopolises are evolving in other parts of the industrialized world, notably in southeastern England and in Japan between Tokyo and Osaka.

---

[17] See *1970 World Population Data Sheet* (publication of Population Reference Bureau Inc.) and *World Urbanization 1950-1970*, Vol. I (1969).

[18] *Building the American City: Report of the National Commission on Urban Problems* (1969), pp. 40-55. See also "Population Profile of the United States," *E.R.R.*, 1967 Vol. II, pp. 801-822.

[19] See *"Megalopolis: Promise and Problems,"* *E.R.R.*, 1965 Vol. I, pp. 101-120.

WHERE AMERICANS LIVE
(in percentages)

By areas	Total population	Whites	Negroes
Central cities	29.4	26.2	54.0
Suburban rings	35.3	37.5	14.6
Non-metropolitan	35.4	36.3	31.4

SOURCE: Census Bureau 1968 estimates.

The development of big-city suburbs also distinguishes recent urban growth from classic patterns of the past. Roundly criticized by urban planners for their profligate waste of space, the suburbs nonetheless have dominated urban growth patterns in the United States and a handful of industrialized nations for the past half a century. Robert C. Weaver, as Secretary of Housing and Urban Development (1966-68), said that "regardless of the merits or defects of our present suburbs, we shall see more of them." [20] As facilities and opportunities—jobs, schools, housing, police protection, environment—deteriorate in the city, those who can afford to do so flee to the suburbs. A recent survey indicated that only 13 per cent of all urban dwellers actually preferred living in the inner city, in contrast to 22 per cent of those surveyed four years earlier. [21]

Rapid Spread of Suburbs; Decline of Inner City

Inner cities will grow by only 13 per cent between now and 1985, less than 1 per cent a year, while the suburbs will more than double in population, according to projections of the National Commission on Urban Problems. The flight to the suburbs takes the upper and middle classes away from the core of the city, leaving the poor behind. To a large extent, Negroes are the urban poor. Conrad F. Taueber, associate director of the Census Bureau, noted in 1969 that the Negro population of the big cities was increasing by 300,000 a year—100,000 from migration, the rest from natural increase. Between 1960 and 1969, he said, the Negro population of cities grew by 2.6 million, while the white population declined by 2.1 million. Three cities—Gary, Ind., Newark, N.J., and Washington, D.C. —are more than 50 per cent Negro. New Orleans, Richmond,

---

[20] Robert C. Weaver, *Dilemmas of Urban America* (1965), p. 8.

[21] Survey cited in "The Population Challenge of the 70's," *Population Bulletin* (publication of Population Reference Bureau Inc.), February 1970.

Chicago, Philadelphia, St. Louis, Detroit, Cleveland, Baltimore and Oakland are expected to be added to that list by 1985. At that time, three-quarters of all American Negroes will live in metropolitan areas, 58 per cent in the inner cities.

The population movement to the suburbs is affecting the political balance of the country. On the basis of 1970 census results now being compiled, the suburbs are expected to gain 37 seats in the House of Representatives for a total of 129, compared with 100 for the inner city and 144 for rural areas. [22] The combined suburban-central city vote will be much larger than that of the rural areas, but this is small comfort to the beleaguered cities. Increasingly, the new suburbs are making common political cause with the older rural right. They are described frequently as a "white noose" around the neck of the black cities. Paul H. Douglas, a former senator (D Ill., 1949-66), has observed that the "new suburban and rural coalition has significantly limited the ability of urban legislators to change the nature of statutes and programs which affect the central city.... This...exacts a subsidy from the central city by imprisoning low-income families and poor families in the central city and sharply limits the dispersion of low-income families to the suburbs."

A *New York Times* reporting team described in the newspaper May 17, 1970, a mood of dismay, sometimes despair, among leaders in five cities the newsmen had visited—Birmingham, Detroit, Philadelphia, San Antonio and Seattle. Local officials accused state and federal governments of failing to help the cities. Mayor A.J. Cervantes of St. Louis was quoted as saying that when he asked Gov. Warren E. Hearnes of Missouri for help, the governor responded with "a call for 'creative localism'."

"The cities probably will be the number one domestic problem of the 1970s," a news executive of United Press International, H. L. Stevenson, told a conference of editors and publishers in October 1969. Some urbanologists believe that suburbs are taking on a commercial life quite independent of the central city. Alexander Ganz, an expert on city planning, predicted in the January 1970 issue of *Technological Review* magazine that within 15 years the prevailing home-to-work pattern will not be from the suburb to the city but from suburb to suburb.

---

[22] The remaining 62 congressional districts cannot be labeled as solely rural, suburban or inner city. See *CQ Weekly Report*, Nov. 21, 1969, pp. 2341-2346.

Future Survival in an Urban Environment

MAN HAS PROVED exceedingly adaptable to city living but there are signs that he has begun to reach the breaking point. "Solutions" to the problems of urban living are almost as numerous as urbanologists and politicians. Suggestions for the future range from a ban by cities on all newcomers, to federal programs for dispersing the nation's population. In recent decades, scores of urban philosophers have come forth, most of them with sweeping visions of the city as man's ideal place of abode.

Paolo Soleri, an Italian architect, wants to build mile-high cities—"arcologies." Another dreamer of urban dreams is Constantine Doxiadis, founder of a city-planning discipline he named "ekistics," from the Greek word for household. He tours the world explaining his concept of building "smallness within size"—clusters of individual communities forming the city as a whole. Doxiadis foresees the emergence of an "ecumenopolis," a world city, in the long future. He explained in his book *Ekistics* (1968) that he seeks the transformation of human attitudes toward cities as much as the reformation of cities. *Fortune* magazine in October 1968 characterized the Doxiadis approach as "a bracingly Olympian view, stretching across great expanses of space and time, but it leaves us with the question of what to do until the ekistician comes."

On the other hand, R. Buckminster Fuller, the inventor and architect, seeks to "reform the environment instead of trying to reform man." [23] In Japan, architect Kenzo Tange has drawn up a master plan for Tokyo that envisions tearing down the city and starting all over again. Tange explained: "There is only one way to save Tokyo and that is to create a new urban structure, a new spatial order, in which the urban system, the traffic system, and the architectural system are organically unified. We have proposed that the antiquated radial structure of Tokyo be replaced by an elongated linear axis of communication, to be developed out across Tokyo Bay." [24]

---

[23] R. Buckminster Fuller, "The Age of Astro Architecture," *Saturday Review*, July 13, 1968, p. 17.

[24] Quoted by Sandy Koffler, "Kenzo Tange and the Megalopolis of Tomorrow," *UNESCO Courier*, September-October, 1968, pp. 54-60.

In Washington, talk centers on rehabilitating existing cities to make them fit for human habitation. Urban renewal has been an aim of the federal government since 1949. It covers a wide range of activities: slum clearance and rebuilding, remodeling of existing structures, improvement of public transportation, expansion of educational systems, and aiding in what was once described as the war on poverty.

Efforts to Renew Cities; Federal Urban Policy

At its best, it can fully engage the efforts of private enterprise in partnership with public agencies to benefit the slum dweller. [25] But there is mounting skepticism that the limited urban renewal programs can have much impact on the problems of the cities. Urban renewal has been attacked in the ghetto as "Negro removal" and in academia as an often-misguided concept which destroys the fabric of the urban neighborhood. Disillusionment with urban renewal shows in almost all professional writing on the subject. One reason for the general frustration with renewal programs is their slow pace. Two years after the riots of April 1968 in Washington, D.C., burned-out stores remained in ruins despite repeated federal promises of rebuilding aid. In many of the nation's cities, urban renewal frequently ends at the stage of slum clearance; vacant lots, not better housing, is the result.

Swedish economist Gunnar Myrdal has said that the needs of American cities require a "Marshall Plan" approach. He said it might cost a trillion dollars and take a generation to accomplish. Alongside the problem, all proposed solutions seem to pale. Many experts think that a very high order of priority ought to be to pull together the frazzled ends of federal, state and local policy. The disarray is bewildering. When the Office of Economic Opportunity, the anti-poverty agency, attempted to compile a catalogue of federal programs available to cities for use by mayors and other city officials, it found that a mere listing of programs ran to several hundred pages. The diffusion of federal programs is matched only by the fragmentation of local government. The 1962 Census of Governments identified 91,187 local governmental units in the United States: counties, municipalities, townships, special districts and school districts.

The task ahead, anthropologist Margaret Mead has said, entails a "complete reshuffling of local, state and national re-

---

25 See "Private Enterprise in City Rebuilding," *E.R.R.*, 1967 Vol. II, pp. 719-735.

sponsibilities for the quality of life. These responsibilities, she said, would involve "the total population in the total environment, eliminating the division between city and country, and responsibility for 'rural' and 'urban' populations." In the view of urban expert A. James Reichley, what is required is nothing short of "a total program for the reconstruction of our society" to blend the needs of the cities along with other urgent demands. [26]

But a number of observers think it is unlikely that this could ever come to pass. Edward Banfield, professor of urban government at Harvard and author of the controversial book *The Unheavenly City* (1970), expresses doubt that government can solve the urban crisis, or even bring about substantive changes. He looks largely to fortuitous "accidental forces," such as rising prosperity or shifts in the demographic composition of the nation, to alter present patterns of urban deterioration. Alan K. Campbell and Jesse Burkhead argue that an "overrising urban policy" will never exist. "The American decision process simply does not work that way. Policy changes are incremental, not sweeping." [27] The strongest argument for a unified federal policy is that otherwise cities are destined to slide into chaos.

Emergence of Planned Cities and New Towns

If urban specialists are bearish about renewing the central cities, they are bullish about building new cities and towns. To the planner, frustrated by the complexities of the decaying inner city, a new town is a *tabula rasa*, a clean slate on which he can make his doodles. Among government officials, Vice President Spiro T. Agnew is enthusiastic about this prospect. "The concept of a new city," he wrote in the introduction to the report of the National Committee on Urban Growth Policy, "offers us a chance to discover what we really want from an urban environment, and what we plan to bring to it... The constant growth of our population confronts us with a desperate race against time if we are to preserve our environment and keep our culture from disintegrating."

"What we really need," one observer said, "is to build whole new cities, rather than new towns. Then we can tackle the problems of race, discrimination, segregation, education,

---

[26] A. James Reichley, "The Political Containment of the Cities," *The States and the Urban Crisis* (1970), p. 195.

[27] Campbell and Burkhead, "Public Policy for Urban America," *Issues in Urban Economics* (edited by Harvey S. Perloff and Lowdon Wingo, 1968), p. 590.

poverty, pollution and traffic congestion."[28] Secretary of Commerce Maurice H. Stans argues that if Americans do not build new cities, and a large number of them, they are inviting an "anthill society." A number of social scientists agree that only new cities will arrest the spread of megalopolis. Athelstan Spilhaus has proposed the erection of an experimental new town of 250,000 persons specifically to test new "far out" methods of design and construction. A San Francisco Bay Area planner, Daniel C. Cook, has proposed a planned community, Cosmopolitas, for one million people. It could be duplicated at 100 sites around the nation. (The equivalent of 12 cities of 250,000 population are built in the United States each year, but in a haphazard manner by adding onto and patching up existing metropolitan areas.)

The new towns most frequently cited as models for urban planners are Vallingby and Farsta, on the outskirts of Stockholm, Sweden; Tapiola, near Helsinki, Finland; and the circle of settlements just outside London's greenbelt. As many as 200 new towns are said to be under construction or in planning in the United States. Some of them in the United States and abroad are conceived as self-contained units, attracting industry, providing jobs and making it unnecessary for residents to work elsewhere. In practice, it rarely works out that way. William H. Whyte noted that there were 9,000 jobs in Vallingby, but most of the people who held them did not live in Vallingby; they commuted to them. The bulk of the wage earners who lived in Vallingby, 25,000 of 27,000, commuted outward, mostly to the center of Stockholm. "In varying degrees, this mixed commutation pattern is true of most new towns in any modern industrial society and it is hard to see how it could be otherwise."[29] New towns are generally close to existing cities. As the suburbs expand outward, they bring the new towns into the metropolitan complex. This is happening to Reston, Va., and Columbia, Md., two new towns on the fringes of Washington.

Not all urban experts are enchanted with the new towns. Whyte dismisses the idea of self-containment as "an impossible vision." He goes on: "As elements of the metropolis, new towns could not take care of more than a fraction of our future population growth, even under the best of circum-

---

28 Franziska P. Hosken, "New Cities for People," *Christian Science Monitor,* Jan. 27, 1969.
29 William H. Whyte, *The Last Landscape,* (1968), p. 267. See also "New Towns," *E.R.R.,* 1968 Vol. II, pp. 805-821.

stances; nor could they significantly change the structure of the metropolis. The English new towns have not; the Scandinavian new towns were never meant to."

A handful of genuine, self-contained new cities are being built around the world. These include Brasilia (Brazil); Islamabad (Pakistan); Chandigarh (Punjab, India); and Ciudad Guayana (Venezuela). It is worth noting that none was built in response to conditions in existing cities, or to alleviate urban problems. Rather, the first three are single-purpose cities, political capitals, built to contain the seat of government. The last is an industrial city, designed to exploit the mineral riches of Venezuela's Guayana region, and to tap the power potential of the swift-flowing Caroni River.

None of these cities is immune to the social problems of older cities. The slums of Brasilia are not as imposing as those of Rio de Janeiro, but they do exist, to the acute embarrassment of the designers of the city. Unemployment in Ciudad Guayana is as high as in Caracas, and rapid migration into the city poses major problems of housing, transportation, education and health services.

New View of Population Control and of Resources

Debate on urban policy inevitably returns to the population question. "Cities are people," Sophocles observed. A solution of the urban problem awaits a decline in the rate people are multiplying on Earth. The present world population of 3.5 billion will double in the next 30 years, demographers forecast. "If present trends continue, we will add a billion people to the world population every five years or less in the 21st century, a detail that the Buck Rogers stories have neglected to mention." [30]

A remarkable shift has taken place in public opinion and government policy on population in recent years. A little more than a decade ago, federal aid for population and family planning was *tabu*. Now, population strategy forms an integral part of this country's foreign assistance programs [31] and is penetrating domestic policy as well. In July 1969, President Nixon sent a set of proposals on population to Congress, the first such legislative message from a Chief Executive in history.

---

[30] Roger O. Egeberg (Assistant Secretary of Health, Education and Welfare), speech to the annual meeting of Planned Parenthood-World Population Inc., Oct. 30, 1969.

[31] U.S. Agency for International Development, *Population Program Assistance: Aid to Developing Countries by the United States, Other Nations, and International and Private Agencies* (1969).

In March 1970, the President signed a bill creating a National Commission on Population Growth and the American Future, and he appointed John D. Rockefeller III as chairman.

Outside the United States, similar shifts in policy and development strategy have occurred. The government of Ghana announced in 1969 a national population program, including demographic research, and dissemination of family planning techniques and birth control information. Catholic bishops of the Philippine Islands and Puerto Rico have given qualified endorsement to state-supported family planning programs for the first time.

At the level of international agencies, the United Nations has initiated a technical assistance program in family planning for member states. World Bank President Robert S. McNamara, who calls excessive population growth "the greatest single obstacle to the economic and social advancement of the majority of peoples in the underdeveloped world," has established a Population Projects Department. In an address to the Bank's board of governors in the fall of 1969, McNamara set new priorities for Bank action in the areas of urbanization, unemployment and industrialization. "The urban population in the developing countries," McNamara said, "has been increasing at an average annual rate of 5 per cent; industrial employment has risen much more slowly." Twenty per cent of the entire male labor force in the developing world is unemployed, he said, and added:

> In the developed countries, rapid economic growth implies full employment. But in the developing countries this is not necessarily the case. Venezuela and Jamaica, for example, both enjoyed average growth rates of 8 per cent a year between 1950 and 1960, but at the end of the decade in Venezuela, unemployment was higher than at the beginning; and in Jamaica it was just as high, in spite of the fact that fully 11 per cent of the labor force had emigrated from the country....

> The cities of the developing countries are the centers which ought to serve as the basis of both industrial growth and social change. Instead, with a growing proportion of their inhabitants living at the very margin of existence, and the quality of life deteriorating for all, the cities are spawning a culture of poverty that threatens the economic health of entire nations.

Despite the turnaround in policy, the battle for population control has barely begun. If population planning were to be applied on a universal scale today, it would have little effect before the end of the century. The parents of the next 3.5 billion humans are, by and large, already born, and ready to reproduce at rates equaling or exceeding those of their own parents. Supporters of the present movement to achieve "Zero Population Growth"—including presidential science adviser Lee A. DuBridge—readily confess that their hopes for success lie decades ahead.

Until quite recently, population problems were clothed in a neo-Malthusian cloak. World food supply was seen as the chief limiting factor to the expanding population. Recent agricultural advances in a number of developing countries [32] have alleviated the threat of famine. But almost nothing has been done to resolve unemployment or onrushing urbanization. There are critics of the "population crisis mentality." But even they admit that population growth must level off sooner or later. From Calcutta to the Boswash megalopolis, the rejoinder is "not sooner, not later—but now."

---

[32] See "Green Revolution," *E.R.R.*, 1970 Vol. I, pp. 221-238.

Stress in Modern Life

by

William Gerber

MENTAL STRESS: ITS CAUSES AND EFFECTS
Emotional Strains Arising From Age of Turmoil
Competitive Urge and Other Causes of Anxiety
Varied Physical and Mental Reactions to Stress
Behavioral Effects: Withdrawal and Aggression

PROGRESS TOWARD UNDERSTANDING STRESS
Knowledge of Psychosomatic Aspects of Stress
Freud's Views on Stress and Human Response
Theories About Peace of Mind and Relaxation
Activities of Sensitivity and Encounter Groups

SEARCH FOR WAYS TO COPE WITH STRESS
Letting Off Steam in Mental and Physical Ways
Building Up Resilience Through Ego Strength
Finding Balance Between Ambition and Repose

1 9 7 0
July 15

STRESS IN MODERN LIFE

CONDITIONS OF STRESS face us no matter which way we turn. War, crime, revolt of youth, drug use, sex problems, crowding, crises at home and at work—all these things produce tension, frustration and harassment at a level that often approaches the threshold of toleration. W. H. Auden calls our era the age of anxiety. Others use labels like rat race and the "stoned age"[1] to describe our society and these times. The average citizen's hopes for a serene life are blasted time and again. Cherished values are battered, religious leaders give currency to Nietzsche's notion that God is dead, computers depersonalize many of life's interchanges, and doctors generate moral complexities by prolonging life artificially and transplanting human organs. Alienation increases and the problems of attaining peace, justice, orderly change and a clean environment grow more complex.

Stress, however, is not all bad. If not excessive, it can serve a useful purpose, such as preparing an individual to meet a threat or fulfilling his need for adventure. Even extreme stress can be constructive if it enables an individual to act effectively for survival. Samuel Silverman, a psychiatrist, contends that stress is not only useful but necessary. "A certain amount of stimulation and excitation—of the right kind and under the right conditions—appears to be necessary for the maintenance of a healthy 'psychophysical tone'."[2] Stress stimulates physical and mental work, helping the person challenge difficult problems.

Stress is thought to be needed even for the ordinary pleasures of living. Dr. Harry J. Johnson, a prominent mental hygienist, contends that "Life without stress is like soup without salt."[3] Moreover, the physiological side effects of pleasur-

---

[1] In reference to the drug culture. Dr. Leo E. Hollister of the Stanford University School of Medicine spoke in 1962 of the "age of tranquilizers," a coinage updating the "aspirin age" of the 1920s. See "Heroin Addiction," *E.R.R.*, 1970 Vol. I, pp. 385-402.

[2] Samuel Silverman (assistant clinical professor of psychiatry at Harvard University), *Psychological Aspects of Physical Symptoms* (1968), p. 393.

[3] Harry J. Johnson, *Eat, Drink, Be Merry and Live Longer* (1968), p. 40.

able stress need not be harmful. Dr. Hans Selye, a professor of psychology at McGill University, wrote that "A game of tennis or even a passionate kiss can produce considerable stress without conspicuous damage.[4] Chicago psychoanalyst Karen Horney has explored the shadow area between good and harmful stress. "Riding a roller-coaster with some apprehension may make it more thrilling," she observed, "whereas doing it with strong anxiety will make it a torture."[5] The achievement in our lives of a beneficial and not excessive exposure to stress requires a deeper knowledge than most people have of themselves and the challenges they face. It requires a knowledge of the causes and effects of stress, of the machinery by which the body and mind attempt to cope with stress, and of controls and outlets.

Competitive Urge and Other Causes of Anxiety

When stress is severe enough to cause an ulcer it may come from man's exaggerated impulse to outdo his peers. This competitive impulse is deeply rooted in Western man. Lennart Levi, director of the Stockholm Laboratory for Clinical Stress Research, wrote:

> The status race begins very often in the nursery. The child is trained as early as possible to control his bodily functions; to sit on his pot, to eat and dress by himself, not when he is biologically prepared for these things but simply as early as possible. The race continues at school...not so much because of the knowledge involved as for the sake of the appropriate certificate, which will serve as a means of further competition.... The competition becomes still more intense in working life.[6]

The Life Extension Institute, headed by Dr. Johnson, found however that "excessive tension among executives is not nearly as prevalent as is commonly supposed." Of 6,000 businessmen polled by the institute, only 13 per cent complained of excessive tension. The others said that they were not working too hard and they liked their jobs very much. Of the 13 per cent who said they suffered from stress, many habitually bolted their food, failed to get regular physical exercise, had no outside interests, and took shortened vacations. Dr. Johnson commented: "Most people are not victims of the rat race. They have created a rat race of their own."

Earning a living involves other causes of stress besides an exaggerated impulse to acquire status. A breadwinner may

---

[4] Hans Selye, *The Stress of Life* (1956), p. 53.
[5] Karen Horney, *The Neurotic Personality of Our Time* (1937), p. 57.
[6] Lennart Levi, *Stress; Sources, Management, and Prevention* (translated by Patrick Hort, 1967), p. 92.

COMMON CAUSES OF STRESS

Stressful aspects of earning a living

Husband-wife incompatibility

Lack of sexual self-confidence

Problems of raising children

Feeling of failure as a spouse, parent, or other family member

Frustration in corresponding with a computerized billing department

Sense of powerlessness against the establishment

Fear of crime

Discrimination by those on a higher level in the social pecking order

Failure to achieve one's ambitions

Health worries

Loss of hope after long continuance of a threat to life or limb

Loss of loved ones

Disruption of patterns of life and social relationships

Indignation over the tactics of those whose political views differ from one's own

Emotional involvement in war-peace issues

Feelings of guilt

Effort to face reality

Natural disasters

Accidents

Combat

---

suffer also from noise at work, personality conflicts with his boss, loss of individuality in a big corporation, fear of losing his job, or even the exasperation of traveling to and from work. A writer has ascribed the rudeness of New Yorkers largely to stress in their daily travel: "Tensions on the subways. Predatory motorists and aggressive pedestrians. Argumentative cab drivers. Honking horns.... Clash. Anger. Hostility."[7] The worries of earning a living do not end at the close of the work day. At home, the breadwinner may grapple with rising food prices, a scarcity of housing that he can afford, and the burden of taxes.

Causes of stress are many and varied, sometimes obvious and sometimes obscure. Some theorists say that sex problems are preponderant; others accord priority to unconscious feelings of guilt or a sense of powerlessness. Some hold, moreover, that stress is most oppressive among well-educated city dwellers. Alex Inkeles, a professor of sociology at Harvard University, has studied the question of whether stress is more aggravated in city life than it is in rural areas. He and his staff interviewed 6,000 urban and rural residents in Argentina, Chile, India, Israel, Nigeria and Pakistan. On the basis of the interviews, he concluded that, at least in developing countries, exposure to modernization and rapid social change was associated with a

---

[7] Michael T. Kaufman, "Rudeness Traced to Rising Stresses Among New Yorkers," *New York Times*, March 2, 1970, p. 33.

decrease—not an increase—in psychosomatic symptoms. The life of the rural dweller, moreover, was far from being disturbance-free. The investigators found that, typically, the peasant is assailed by stressful conditions because of his dependence on "the benevolence of a landlord and the capriciousness of the climate."[8]

Varied Physical and Mental Reactions to Stress

Perhaps the best-known description of what happens organically when stress occurs has been provided by Hans Selye. Defining stress as "the rate of all the wear and tear caused by life," Selye divides human response to stress into three stages: (1) alarm, including a "report" to the endocrine glands; (2) resistance, with the aid of stepped-up production of adrenal hormones; and (3) exhaustion, collapse, or relaxation after the stressful assault has subsided.[9] Sigmund Freud, years earlier, theorized on mental reaction to stress. (See page 536)

Richard S. Lazarus, professor of psychology at the University of California at Berkeley, sees a four-part development—not so much in terms of the body's defense reaction, as Selye outlined, but in terms of what happens in the individual both mentally and physically after the onset of stress. One part of the response consists of emotional disturbance—fear, anxiety, anger, or depression. Another consists of motor-behavioral patterns such as facial expressions, gritted teeth, or folded arms, and either flight or attack. A third has to do with bodily changes—secretions of adrenal hormones and increases in the heart rate, blood pressure, skin temperature, and sweating. Last, but not in chronological order, there are disturbances in cognitive functioning caused by a degree of shock. Usually this results in an impairment of skilled performance, perception, learning and judgment, but sometimes performance and perception are actually heightened.

When does stress cause improved performance, and when does it cause impairment? While Lazarus found no easy answers to the question, it may be said that mild or moderate stress often facilitates performance while severe stress usually impairs performance. Complex tasks involving great concentration are far more vulnerable to the effects of stress than are simple, repetitive tasks. What type of person improves his performance under stress is not yet known.[10]

---

[8] Interview with Inkeles, *New York Times*, May 26, 1970, p. 22.

[9] "Selye's stress theory [is] one of the 20th century's milestone research achievements."—J. D. Ratcliff, "How to Avoid Harmful Stress," *Today's Health*, July 1970, p. 42.

[10] Richard S. Lazarus, "Stress," *International Encyclopedia of the Social Sciences* (1968), Vol. 15, p. 339.

In his book *Six Crises* (1962), Richard M. Nixon analyzed his own reaction to stress in trying situations. He wrote: "When a man has been through even a minor crisis, he learns not to worry when his muscles tense up, his breathing becomes faster, his nerves tingle, his stomach churns, his temper becomes short, his nights are sleepless. He recognizes such symptoms as the natural and healthy signs that his system is keyed up for battle." Elsewhere in the book, the future President said: "...My experience had been in preparing to meet a crisis, the more I worked the sharper and quicker my mental reactions became. I began to notice, however, the inevitable symptoms of tension...I suppose some might say that I was 'nervous,' but I knew these were simply evidences of preparing for battle."

Psychosomatic effects of stress occur in various guises. Samuel Silverman attributes many headaches, backaches, digestive upsets, states of fatigue, palpitations, pains in all parts of the body to "tensions of the day." Digestive upsets due to stress may take the form of nausea, nervous stomach ("butterflies" in the stomach), constipation, or diarrhea; if prolonged, they can produce an ulcer, considered a badge of honor in some occupations. Sleeplessness as a psychosomatic effect of stress may plague an individual for weeks, months, or years. Severe stress sometimes produces psychological disturbances characterized by self-pity, apathy, or despair. Apathy resulting from stress may lead eventually in either of two directions: to explosive action, especially in association with others, or to suicide.[11]

A group of Copenhagen neurologists recently completed a 23-year study of what happened to Danish survivors of Nazi concentration camps. The victims had been exposed in the camps to hunger, cold, overcrowding, terrorization, and other causes of stress. The long-term effects, which became apparent over the postwar years, included persistent weight loss, frequent fatigue, premature aging, reduced sexual potency, recurrent nightmares, and reduced intellectual capacity. On the basis of the study, Denmark enacted a new law which states that exposure to stress is the only objective criterion for providing compensation to the Nazi camp survivors. "This legislation is a revolutionary departure from the theory that the individual's reaction to stress lies in his own constitution, and not in either the intensity or duration of the stress...."[12]

---

[11] See "Anatomy of Suicide," *E.R.R.*, 1963 Vol. II, pp. 705-706.
[12] H. J. Barnes, "Compensation for Camp Victims," *Science News*, June 20, 1970, p. 604.

In experiments with rats and other animals, overcrowding was found to produce a characteristic pattern of responses that included homosexuality, cannibalism, extreme withdrawal, and other forms of abnormal behavior. This pattern has been labeled "behavioral sink." John B. Calhoun, a psychologist at the National Institute of Mental Health who has studied the effects of overcrowding, believes that there is a close analogy between the behavioral sink pattern in animals and unrest, violence, crime and demoralization in teeming cities.[13]

Some writers have speculated that war is one of the social effects of stress.[14] National leaders have been known to foment war as an outlet for political unrest. But additional psychological or social elements seem to be necessary for stirring the cauldron of war. Among these are ideological differences, nationalism, and the availability of threatening armament on both sides. Some of these ingredients themselves appear to result from stress.

Progress Toward Understanding Stress

THOMAS HOBBES (1588-1679) described the stressful life of man in the state of nature, a state he believed to have preceded the congregation of men in society, as "solitary, poor, nasty, brutish and short." By contrast, Jean-Jacques Rousseau (1712-1778) held that "man is born free" and a "noble savage" until restrained by the stresses of civilized living. Eighteenth-century confidence in the perfectibility of man and society gave way to a mood of pessimism. Arthur Schopenhauer (1788-1860) pictured mankind as doomed to torment and misery. In *Walden*, Henry David Thoreau wrote: "The mass of men lead lives of quiet desperation."

William Harvey (1578-1657) was the first to recognize an association between mental or physical stress and the rate of pumping of blood by the heart. Another English physician, Thomas Sydenham (1624-1689), found that the root of many physical diseases "cannot be...brought to light by...an exami-

---

[13] See "Urbanization of the Earth," *E.R.R.*, 1970 Vol. I, p. 368.

[14] Theories associating frustration, aggression, the drive for territory, and the drive for domination with war are summarized in Quincy Wright's *A Study of War* (2nd ed., 1965), pp. 131-144.

nation of the body." Philippe Pinel, practicing medicine in Paris, noted in 1798 that some diseases affecting the body are emotional in origin and consequently do not show such causal signs as "inflammation or morbid alteration in structure."

The term "psychosomatic" was invented in 1818 by Johann C. Heinroth, a German medical researcher, to describe the physical effects of mental disturbances. Conceptual schemes aimed at explaining the effect of hysteria on the body were developed by Jean M. Charcot (1825-1893) and Pierre Janet (1859-1947), as well as by Sigmund Freud (1856-1939). Psychosomatic medicine achieved prominence in the United States in the 1930s, when the physical toll exacted by stress and tension became more noticeable throughout the nation than it had been before.

Some doctors believe that two of every three patients seeking medical advice suffer psychosomatically. In a study of patients with congestive heart failure admitted to the Cincinnati General Hospital, approximately 75 per cent had recently undergone an emotional crisis, such as a death or divorce in the family or a severe financial loss. Recent findings suggest that even infectious diseases can be psychosomatic. Two medical researchers found that the stress pigs undergo in being transported to market tended to activate latent salmonella infection in the animals. The two concluded that their findings, together with other research, supports the hypothesis that man also "may behave in this way."[15]

However, physician Robert C. Page discounts the belief that stress alone produces illness in humans. "It is not hard work, nor even stress, that makes trouble for the ulcer-prone individual. It is gnawing unhappiness, unrelieved distress, dissatisfaction with personal limitations and a compulsion to go beyond them, or a feeling of guilt over having knuckled under to them that will trigger the stomach reaction."[16]

Freud's Views on Stress and Human Response

Sigmund Freud, in the early years of his practice, treated a number of patients who, as a psychosomatic effect of anxiety, were paralyzed physically in some part of the body or had a sensory organ that did not function. Freud began to ponder about the machinery whereby the mind reacts to stressful experiences and churns out abnormal behavioral responses. He reached the conclusion that life's incessant frustrations are

---

[15] Leslie P. Williams Jr. and Kenneth W. Newell, "Salmonella Excretion in Joy-Riding Pigs," *American Journal of Public Health*, May 1970, p. 928.

[16] Robert C. Page, M.D., *How to Lick Executive Stress* (1967), p. 92.

a direct cause of neurosis: "The most immediate, most easily discerned and most comprehensible exciting cause of the onset of neurotic illness lies in that external factor which may generally be described as frustration."[17]

Freud was one of the first to develop a theoretical model of what happens when an individual is subjected to stress. First, he said, there is danger or a threat. Anxiety ensues. Finally, the individual puts into action his defenses against anxiety. The defense mechanisms, of which one or more may be activated, are avoidance, denial and repression, which may include "active forgetting"; rationalization, or finding reasons to support a preconception needed for peace of mind; projection of one's own feeling of distress onto someone else, as when a patient plagued by his compulsion to dominate deems his doctor morbidly domineering; sublimation, or diversion of a blocked sexual urge into artistic, intellectual, or philanthropic channels; and regression, or reverting to childishness.

Freud's theories had little influence in studies of stress-induced mental aberration during World War I. Psychologists and physicians then believed that what was called shell shock was a manifestation of brain damage resulting from explosion of shells nearby. The term commonly used in World War II, battle fatigue, reflected fuller recognition of emotional factors, as distinguished from physiological, and fuller acceptance of Freudian theories. Questions remain in evaluating human reaction to stress on the battlefield. These questions have entered into military trials of American servicemen accused by their government of committing atrocities in Viet Nam.

Theories About Peace of Mind and Relaxation

In recent years, psychoanalysts have extended Freud's list of defense mechanisms to include eating, drinking, gum-chewing, smoking, and drug-taking; irrational laughter, weeping, and cursing; sleeping; fantasizing; and fanatical devotion to physical exercise. Freudians also joined forces in some cases with existentialist thinkers who attributed mental woes to the irrationality of the human condition. Jean-Paul Sartre and other existentialists hold that life is characterized by anxiety resulting from the absurdity of things as well as from man's freedom, and necessity, to create his own essence by whatever he decides to do. Existentialist psychoanalysts have tried to open up neurotic minds to realization of these conditions of life, believing that such realization is a step toward coping with stress.[18]

---

[17] "Types of Neurotic Nosogenesis," in *A General Selection from the Works of Sigmund Freud* (edited by John Rickman, 1937), p. 70.

[18] See "Future of Psychiatry," *E.R.R.*, 1969 Vol. I, pp. 137-138.

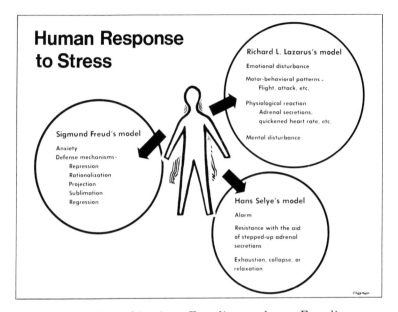

Human Response to Stress

Richard L. Lazarus's model

Emotional disturbance

Motor-behavioral patterns - Flight, attack, etc.

Physiological reaction Adrenal secretions, quickened heart rate, etc.

Mental disturbance

Sigmund Freud's model

Anxiety
Defense mechanisms -
 Repression
 Rationalization
 Projection
 Sublimation
 Regression

Hans Selye's model

Alarm

Resistance with the aid of stepped-up adrenal secretions

Exhaustion, collapse, or relaxation

The work of psychiatrists, Freudian and non-Freudian, was supplemented after World War II by the writings of persons who developed prescriptions for cultivating peace of mind and relaxation. Rabbi Joshua L. Liebman and Bishop Fulton J. Sheen, respectively, wrote *Peace of Mind* (1946) and *Peace of Soul* (1949). Combining the scientific and popular approaches, George S. Stevenson, a physician, wrote *Master Your Tensions and Enjoy Living Again* (1959). He prescribed the following measures for self-administered therapy in periods of stress: talk it out, escape for a while, work off your anger, give in occasionally, do something for others, take one thing at a time, shun the superman urge, go easy with criticism, give the other fellow a break, make yourself available to others who need you, and schedule your recreation.

Many people in the 1950s and 1960s sought inner peace in the face of life's stresses by methods originating in the Orient. Zen Buddhism and Hindu meditation attracted young people who were willing to try exercises in mental concentration as a path to peace of mind. Similar motivations prompted some to become devotees of the occult.[19]

People troubled by the stress of life began to receive treatment in groups in the early years of this century. In the 1920s, Viennese psychiatrist Jacob L. Moreno introduced in the United States the psychodrama, a procedure in which patients

---

[19] See "The Occult vs. the Churches," *E.R.R.*, 1970 Vol. I, pp. 301-303, and "Eastern Religions and Western Man," *E.R.R.*, 1969 Vol. I, pp. 435-438.

play such roles as that of a sales clerk fearful of losing his job, the clerk's wife, his employer, and a customer. Group therapy is based on the supposition that each participant may get relief by becoming aware of another's troubles and by ventilating his own.

Activities of Sensitivity and Encounter Groups

Group meetings for individuals who wished to improve their ability to cope with stress began after World War II when the National Training Laboratory at Bethel, Maine, organized training groups ("T-groups") for enhancing the human relations skills of supervisors. This work came to be called sensitivity training. Other institutions besides the one at Bethel which conduct sensitivity training include the Human Development Institute at Atlanta, a subsidiary of Bell and Howell Co., and the American Behavioral Training Laboratories at Detroit, owned by former rent-a-car magnate Warren Avis.

Among the companies that have sent executives to T-groups are General Electric Co., Honeywell Inc., Aerojet-General Corp., Humble Oil and Refining Co., and U.S. Plywood-Champion Papers Inc. Some have begun to phase out their participation, especially in the light of recent criticism of the groups. Alan N. Schoonmaker, an industrial psychologist, wrote: "There is no solid evidence that T-groups and similar programs improve organizational effectiveness." And Thomas Meehan, a social commentator, said: "The theory behind sensitivity training...is that the brute who enters the program with all the sensitivity of a defense lineman for the Baltimore Colts will emerge with the quivering nerves of a lyric poet."[20]

Several kinds of sensitivity programs stemmed from the T-groups. One is the encounter group, considered by counseling expert Carl R. Rogers the most important social invention of the century. The best known of the organizations which conduct encounter groups is the Esalen Institute at Big Sur, Calif. It was established in the 1950s and had about 25,000 participants in 1969. A session at the institute may consist of both sexes appearing in the nude, seated hip-deep in a shallow swimming pool. Participants might express themselves by screaming, touching someone's face, pushing, or staring in another's eyes.[21]

---

[20] Thomas Meehan, "The Flight from Reason," *Horizon*, Spring 1970, p. 8; Alan N. Schoonmaker, *Anxiety and the Executive* (1969), p. 212.

[21] Jane Howard, *Please Touch; A Guided Tour of the Human Potential Movement* (1970), pp. 9-17.

Several thousand encounter groups were operating in the United States in the spring of 1970, including about 5,000 in New York City and about 200 in and near Palo Alto, Calif.[22] Bob Kriegel, 32-year-old director of Anthos, a New York City group, told an interviewer: "New Yorkers need this kind of release more than anyone else. There is so much hostility here, so much outside bombardment of stimuli—the noise, traffic, the crowds, television—that people have totally lost contact with themselves....People are afraid to stop and find out who they are."[23] A special kind of encounter group is aimed at enabling militant blacks and policemen, teachers and students, representatives of labor and management, and other hostile or potentially hostile groups to get to know each other.

The American Psychiatric Association was told in May 1970 that while encounter groups may benefit some persons, they are potentially dangerous to others who might be on the brink of a breakdown. An association task force headed by Dr. Irvin D. Yalon of Stanford University had this to say in a report *(Encounter Groups and Psychiatry):* "They [encounter groups] subject people to an intense emotional experience. That's going to be difficult for people handling severe stress." The report added that the leader of an encounter group should be trained by a recognized institute and know how to recognize abnormal stress in a participant. Yalon warned against "weekend messiahs who go through an [encounter group] experience, hang out a shingle and begin running their own group."

Search for Ways to Cope With Stress

ALVIN TOFFLER, of the Russell Sage Foundation fears that "We are creating an environment so filled with astonishments, twists, reversals, eruptions, mind-jangling crises, and innovations as to test the limits of man's adaptive capacity."—"We are setting the stage for future shock on a vast scale."[24] Some

[22] In the early months of 1970, the New York organization known as GROW (Group Relations Ongoing Workshops) was charging $960 for one year of six encounters a week, or $1,600 for one year of 10 encounters a week. A participant who completes either of these courses receives a certificate stating that he is authorized to lead a group himself.

[23] Linda Francke, "See Me, Feel Me, Touch Me, Heal Me: The Encounter Group Explosion," *New York*, May 25, 1970, p. 36.

[24] Alvin Toffler, "Future Shock," *Horizon*, Spring 1970, p. 82—an article adapted from Toffler's book *Coping With Future Shock* (1970).

psychologists and social scientists believe that stress in social relations could be eased by decreasing the size of institutions, communities and governments. There are others who believe that tighter law enforcement would promote the order and security needed for a relaxation of anxieties in urban America. Still others maintain that if the government provided more help to the less privileged it would reduce stress caused by deprivation or discrimination.

Some young people have rejected material success as a primary goal in life. They tend to "hang loose" in a job and face stress with equanimity. Other youths reject the earning of money through a regular job because they consider that way of living to be cursed with the stress of competitiveness.[25] Young people, with renewable wellsprings of energy, may be better equipped to cope with stress than their elders.

A multitude of Americans, young and old, have made alcohol and drugs their response to pressures encountered in everyday life. Studies conducted by the National Institute of Mental Health show that nearly one-half of the American adult population has taken mood-changing drugs. And hundreds of thousands of young people are experimenting with amphetamines, marijuana and other drugs in an effort—ultimately unsuccessful—to cope with stress.

"To get physically tired," heart specialist Paul Dudley White said, "is the best antidote for nervous tension."[26] Play tennis, chop wood, punch a bag—any number of fatiguing activities are good for releasing belligerent impulses aroused by the stress of living. Yelling at the umpire or even watching a violence-filled movie may also provide outlets for aggressive impulses. Aristotle said that attending a tragic drama purges the soul of its tensions by arousing and then exhausting pity and fear.

Building Up Resilience Through Ego Strength

Seeking an unrelated outlet for one's frustrations is not always the best therapy, however. It may be beneficial for the person to acknowledge the stresses that afflict him and try to work around them. Erik Erikson contends that we should confront our anxieties. The first step is "to train our fear...to remain an accurate measure and warning of that which man

---

[25] See "Communal Living," *E.R.R.*, 1969 Vol. II, pp. 577-578, 594.
[26] Quoted in "Tension, Anxiety, and Nervous Distress: How to Cope With Everyday Pressures," *Better Homes and Gardens*, April 1967, p. 26.

must fear."[27] Terence Moore, psychologist of London's Child Guidance Training Center, wrote:

> This quality of resilience apparently varies from birth, and very probably has a genetic component; but it seems likely, too, that it may be fostered or reduced by environmental conditions, especially in the early years. Adults can sometimes show children how to cope successfully with everyday stresses. Or lacking understanding or sympathy, they can very easily undermine the child's efforts and increase the stress to the breaking point, when tears or a tantrum will result.[28]

Resilience depends partly on ego strength, or self-esteem. Psychologists and social workers in recent years have developed a technique for bolstering the ego resources of persons undergoing severe stress. This technique, called crisis intervention, is applied especially to people who appear to be heading for a breakdown because of bereavement, fear of surgery, or other identifiable causes. Visits by close friends, reassurance, encouragement, praise, explanations, and opportunities for a good cry are parts of the technique.

Crisis intervention to promote resilience in periods of stress has been tried also in cases of social turmoil. During the time of riots that tore many other American cities in 1968, Mayor John V. Lindsay made himself visible in ghetto areas of New York, offering needed support that encouraged people to mourn instead of riot. In Boston, at the request of Mayor Kevin White, soul-singer James Brown stayed on television to serve as a calming influence. Brown also appeared later on radio and television in Washington for the same purpose.

Finding Balance Between Ambition and Repose

A complete absence of stress is not an admirable ideal. As Hans Selye noted in *The Stress of Life* (1956): "Comfort and security make it easier for us to enjoy the good things in life, but they are not, in themselves, great and enjoyable aims." Even as a temporary measure for therapeutic purposes, the absence of stress is not necessarily a wise goal. Selye wrote: "I have always been against the advice of physicians who would send a high-strung, extremely active business executive to a long, enforced exile in some health resort, with a view of relieving him from stress by absolute inactivity."

A balance between ambition and repose would seem to be desirable, but there are exceptions. Eugene E. Levitt, a pro-

---

[27] Erik Erikson, *Childhood and Society* (second edition, 1964), p. 407.
[28] Terence Moore, "Stress in Normal Childhood," *Human Relations,* June 1969, p. 235.

fessor of clinical psychology, said: "We can only wonder vainly what De Quincy or Poe or Van Gogh would have produced if they had been emotionally better balanced."[29] Selye's suggestion is that one should "live and express his personality at a tempo and in a manner best suited to his inherited talents, under the prevailing social conditions."

One key to achieving a proper balance is the principle of variety. Dr. Johnson offers these suggestions for applying that principle:

> Every desk-bound worker should leave his chair at least once every two hours and walk about his office for a few minutes.
>
> Chairmen should call for occasional ten-minute intermissions during meetings, breaking up both tension and boredom.
>
> Relaxation does not mean rest; it means a change of scene, a change of activity.
>
> The best cure for tension fatigue is walking.

In the Old Testament wisdom of Ecclesiastes, there is a proper season for everything. Thus we should allow a time for ambition and a time for repose. Modern medicine holds that the division between stress and relaxation should apply not only to daily matters but to life as a whole. Plans such as these, unfortunately, have a way of being exploded by stressful events that were not anticipated. Therefore, the individual needs to build two things: a plan for balance between stress and non-stress, and sufficient ego strength to endure the destruction of the plan.

---

[29] Eugene E. Levitt (Indiana University School of Medicine), *The Psychology of Anxiety* (1968), p. 234.

Status of Women

by

Helen B. Shaffer

WOMEN'S DRIVE FOR EQUAL OPPORTUNITY
Revival of Feminist Fervor Through 'Women's Lib'
New Activist Groups; Discrimination Complaints
Tightening of Federal Rules to Prevent Job Bias
Attack on Male Favoritism in Colleges, Churches
Support for Proposed 'Equal Rights' Amendment

WOMEN IN EMPLOYMENT, EDUCATION, POLITICS
Rising Proportion of Working Wives, Mothers
Women's Work: Lower Paid and Less Prestigious
Meager Female Representation in the Professions
Diminishing Number of Women in Elective Posts

ISSUES AND PORTENTS FOR EQUAL RIGHTS
Question of Feminism's Decline After Suffrage
Attempt to Link Women's Cause With Negroes'
Division Over Goals: Equal Rights or Protection
Far-Reaching Influence of New-Style Feminists

STATUS OF WOMEN

A NY CELEBRATION of the 50th anniversary of woman's suffrage in the United States must necessarily be tempered by the realization that the status of women in American society still has a long way to go to reach par with that of men. It was on Aug. 26, 1920, that Secretary of State Bainbridge Colby proclaimed the 19th Amendment to the Constitution granting women the right to vote. Eight days earlier, on Aug. 18, Tennessee had become the 36th state to ratify and thus validate the amendment. Postal officials will acknowledge the historic occasion by issuing on Aug. 26 a commemorative stamp in a special ceremony at Adams, Mass., birthplace of suffragist leader Susan B. Anthony.

More indicative of the anniversary mood, however, is the emergence of the women's liberation movement ("Women's Lib"), bent on finishing the job the suffragists began more than a century ago. Whether or not many women stage a strike or otherwise demonstrate for their rights on Aug. 26, as called for by Now (National Organization for Women) and endorsed by a number of other women's groups, the evidence will still point to a heightened militancy in the continuing struggle to elevate the status of women in American life.

It is a mistake to judge the strength of the new rise of feminism by the relatively small number of women who physically storm male sanctuaries or shout obscenities at male reporters. They are only the outer edge of mounting impatience among women against the secondary role which society has assigned to their sex. Like the Black Panther Party in its relationship to the Negro population, the few militant women awaken deeply buried feelings within large numbers of other women who never before consciously thought of themselves as oppressed.

Women's rights as an issue has rarely interested more than a handful of men, except as a subject for humor. Its resurgence at this time, however, may well herald a considerable change in the American life style affecting men and women alike—certainly more change than followed suffrage a half-century ago. Some observers believe the impact will be even greater than that of the black drive for status. The male editor of *The Ladies' Home Journal,* John Mack Carter, whose office was invaded March 18, 1970, by 200 feminists to voice their complaints about the contents of women's magazines, wrote later that "beneath the shrill accusations and the radical dialectic, our editors heard some convincing truths about the persistence of sexual discrimination." In an introduction to a special section of the August issue of *The Journal* which he turned over to the protesting women, Carter said: "We seemed to catch a rising note of angry self-expression among today's American women, a desire for representation, for recognition, for a broadening range of alternatives in a rapidly changing society." The new movement "may have an impact far beyond its extremist eccentricities."

Advisory boards to the federal government have taken note of the growing feminist fury. Virginia R. Allen, chairman of the President's Task Force on Women's Rights and Responsibilities, told President Nixon: "American women are increasingly aware and restive over the denial of equal opportunity, equal responsibility, equal protection of law." The Citizen's Advisory Council on the Status of Women observed that "a revival of the feminist movement has occurred during the past four years and it is greatly increasing in momentum, especially among younger women."[1]

The new awareness and restiveness of women have been heightened by social unrest and the sexual revolution. Today's feminists are a different breed from their sisters who fought for suffrage. They do not limit themselves to specific goals such as equality in employment. They are mounting an assault on an entrenched pattern of relations between the sexes that, in their eyes, demeans and restricts one-half the human race. It follows that feminist militants are in the vanguard of opposition to abortion laws which they consider a denial of a woman's control over her own body. They are for abolition of alimony for wife support if a divorcee is physically and mentally able to support herself. They are in arms against mass media presentation of women as sexual objects; some women's lib groups are calling for a boycott of products of companies that stress female sexual allure in their advertising. At the ex-

---

[1] Mrs. Allen's remarks were made public June 10, 1970, in a letter to President Nixon accompanying a task force report; the council's words are contained in *The Proposed Equal Rights Amendment to the United States Constitution: A Memorandum,* March 1970. The council was established by executive order of the President in 1963 to advise government agencies; the task force was appointed by the President in September 1969.

treme, they oppose conventional marriage in favor of "voluntary association": motherhood without a husband would become fully acceptable.[2]

New Activist Groups; Discrimination Complaints

Though only a very few women publicly protest their "second sex" status and millions of women obviously have no desire to abandon their traditional role as wife-mother-homemaker, there are signs nevertheless that pressures for equalization are moving forward. For one thing, feminine activism is bringing concrete results. Individual women, often backed by militant feminist organizations, are filing formal complaints against employers, unions, educational institutions, restaurants, and government agencies, charging discrimination against members of their sex. Three relatively new organizations have been particularly effective in bringing pressure on regulatory bodies to act on sex discrimination complaints and in initiating or supporting litigation in the field of women's rights. They are Now, founded in 1966 by Betty Friedan, author of *The Feminine Mystique*,[3] and the still newer WEAL (Women's Equity Action League) and Human Rights for Women, Inc.

Now, based in New York, has 35 chapters around the country and claims 5,000 to 10,000 members. It appeals to discontented housewives as well as to working women and is the nearest thing to a mass organization the new feminism has produced. WEAL is made up chiefly of professional and business women and works largely in the field of legal action. Human Rights for Women, based in Washington, D.C., supplies legal aid in sex discrimination cases. These are traditionally structured organizations with specific goals to be obtained by working within the political system. In addition there are more radical groups, spawned by the New Left and the campus protest movements, which come and go under a variety of names. The best-known among them are Women's Liberation, the Radical Feminists, WITCHES (Women's International Terrorist Conspiracy from Hell) and Redstockings.

Knocking down sex barriers to men's bars may not at first sight seem a great boon to the welfare of womankind. But to the women who brought suit against McSorley's Old Ale

---

[2] See "Sexual Revolution: Myth or Reality," *E.R.R.*, 1970 Vol. I, pp. 241-257, and "Abortion Law Reform," *E.R.R.*, 1970 Vol. II, pp. 545-562.

[3] In *The Feminine Mystique* (1963), often referred to as the bible of the new feminism, Mrs. Friedan denounced the forces in society that keep women in thrall to the ideal of the sexpot and/or perfect housewife.

House in New York, the victory in court provided the satisfaction of laying down a principle. A federal judge ruled on June 25, 1970, that McSorley's, an all-male tavern since its founding in 1854, was a public place subject to the equal protection clause of the Constitution, and hence its exclusion of women customers was unconstitutional. While the ruling was on appeal to higher court, the New York City Council on July 22 enacted an ordinance to prohibit discrimination against women in bars, restaurants, and similar public places. To women of the liberation movement, segregation by sex is like segregation by race—a form of discrimination, damaging economically, socially, and psychologically. And there are many "men only" signs, seen and unseen, that block a woman's way to a good lunch—or a promotion.

Of more immediate benefit to the cause may be the feminist drive against discrimination in employment, which has begun to show results. Approximately one-fourth of the 12,000 charges of discrimination in employment brought before the Equal Employment Opportunity Commission each year involve discrimination because of sex. The commission administers Title VII of the Civil Rights Act of 1964, which forbids discrimination in employment on account of race, color, religion, national origin, or sex. Under feminist pressure, the commission toughened its stand on the employment rights of women. It voted Aug. 15, 1969, to amend its guidelines so that employers cannot be excused for practices unlawful under the federal act by claiming that those practices conform with state laws. Paradoxically, many of those state laws were enacted originally to protect women in such matters as long hours, night work and physically difficult work. The commission said such laws "have ceased to be relevant to our technology or to the expanding role of the female worker in our economy."

Federal courts in California and Oregon ruled in 1968 and 1969 that state laws protecting women workers were superseded by the sex-discrimination ban in Title VII. Attorneys General in at least six states—Michigan, North Dakota, Oklahoma, Ohio, Pennsylvania and South Dakota—and the Corporation Counsel of the District of Columbia have issued similar opinions in recent months. In several cases the employing firm has taken the initiative in suits to throw out laws limiting women's hours of work.

The U.S. Court of Appeals for the Seventh Circuit (Chicago) ruled on Sept. 26, 1969, that employers may not exclude women from jobs requiring the lifting of 35 pounds or more, but must afford each worker "a reasonable opportunity to demonstrate his or her ability to perform more strenuous jobs."[4] In a similar case the Fifth Circuit Court of Appeals (New Orleans) held that the burden of proof lies on the employer to prove he had "a factual basis for believing that... substantially all women would be unable to perform safely and efficiently the duties of the job involved."[5]

Tightening of Federal Rules to Prevent Job Bias

The Equal Employment Opportunity Commission has taken the position that employers and employment agencies cannot advertise a preference for one sex or the other unless sex is a "bona fide occupational qualification." Such jobs are said to be very few—jobs for actors and washroom attendants perhaps but not nurses or engineers or stewards of ships or planes. The commission issued a guideline on Jan. 24, 1969, holding it unlawful to place ads in "Help Wanted - Male" or "Help Wanted - Female" columns unless sex is genuinely a "bfoq." The American Newspaper Publishers Association and the Washington (D.C.) *Evening Star* have challenged this rule in a court case. Many newspapers have continued the custom of sex-separated Help Wanted columns. Only recently have individual women, moved by the new feminist fervor, begun to file charges on the want ad question.

The Supreme Court in March 1970 decided to review its first case involving a charge of sex discrimination in employment under the 1964 Civil Rights Act. At issue is the validity of a company rule that excluded a mother of young children from a position as assembly-line trainee. The Court will review an appeal from a lower federal court decision favorable to the company, Martin Marietta Corp. The case is of particular interest because G. Harrold Carswell voted with the majority of judges in appellate court who denied a petition for rehearing. When President Nixon later nominated Carswell for the Supreme Court, feminists remembered his vote and accused him of being a "sexist." Rep. Patsy T. Mink (D Hawaii) was among several women who testified against his nomination at Senate Judiciary Committee hearings. The Senate on April 8, 1970, rejected the Carswell nomination, but not on grounds of "sexism."

Complaints of violations of the Equal Pay Act of 1963 rose from 351 in 1965 to approximately 565 in fiscal 1970. Accord-

---

[4] Bowe et al *v.* Colgate Palmolive Co.
[5] Weeks *v.* Southern Bell Telephone and Telegraph Co.

ing to the Department of Labor, which administers this law, an estimated $17 million in back pay is due women workers who have been paid less than men for the same work, contrary to law. The Supreme Court laid down an important principle recently in an equal pay case involving female employees of the Wheaton Glass Co. of Millville, N.J.—that jobs need not be identical but only "substantially equal" for the equal pay rule to apply.[6] A federal district court in Dallas ruled on Oct. 8, 1969, that the traditionally all-male job of hospital orderly was substantially equal to that of the traditionally female job of nurse's aide.[7]

The Department of Justice filed suit on July 20, 1970, against Libbey-Owens-Ford, glass manufacturer, for allegedly discriminating against women in violation of the equal employment provision of the Civil Rights Act. The department asked the U.S. District Court in Toledo, Ohio, to order the company to hire, train, promote, and pay women equally with men in its five Toledo area plants. Despite this landmark action—the first time the Justice Department has gone to court to enforce the sex equality provision—women leaders are critical of alleged foot-dragging by the Nixon administration.

They were cheered on June 10, 1970, when Secretary of Labor James D. Hodgson met feminist demands by releasing guidelines for enforcing executive orders to prohibit sex discrimination by government contractors. The guidelines directed employers not to make any distinction by sex in hiring, wages, hours, or other conditions of employment; in advertising not to specify male or female help unless sex was a bona fide job requirement; not to exclude mothers of young children (unless they also excluded the fathers), not to penalize women who took time off for childbirth, and so on. But disillusionment soon set in. At the insistence of leaders of women's rights groups, Hodgson met with them on July 25 to explain his position. Saying that discrimination against women was "subtle and more pervasive" than against any other group, he added that he had "no intention of applying literally exactly the same approach for women" as for other instances of discrimination in employment. One of the women leaders, Dr. Ann Scott of

---

[6] The Supreme Court on May 18, 1970, confirmed a lower court order requiring the company to pay more than $250,000 back pay to female employees. The Court action also meant that women selector-packers would receive a 21½-cent-an-hour increase. The company had contended that male workers were worth more because they could lift and stack heavy cartons of glass containers.

[7] See Robert D. Moran's analysis, "Reducing Discrimination: Role of the Equal Pay Act," *Monthly Labor Review*, June 1970, pp. 32-33.

Williamsville, N.Y., said after the meeting: "Women have been left out again by the Nixon administration."

Women won a partial victory, however, Hodgson announced on July 31 that "goals and timetables" would be set for employment of women by federal contractors. The goals and timetables were to be determined after the government had consulted with representatives of employers, labor unions, and women's groups. A blanket application of a no-discrimination rule on all jobs was not contemplated. The sex discrimination problem differed from that of race discrimination, Hodgson said, because many women do not seek employment and many jobs sought by minority males do not attract women.

Attack on Male Favoritism in Colleges, Churches

Feminist organizations are beginning to use federal anti-discrimination laws to attack long-standing practices of sex discrimination in higher education. The prevalence of government contract work in universities gives the militants a handle for bringing pressure. Favoritism toward males in hiring faculty members and admitting students to graduate and professional schools henceforth might mean the loss of a government contract. Two of the new women's organizations, Now and WEAL, have taken the lead here. They have named at least 100 colleges and universities in making complaints to federal agencies that administer the university contracts. The *Chronicle of Higher Education* reported in its issue of June 1, 1970, that government investigators had gone to Harvard and several other campuses. Some institutions—the University of Chicago is one—have responded to rising feminist pressure by setting up investigating committees of their own.

Not all of the push is coming from new militant groups. The 88-year-old American Association of University Women has brought a complaint against the U.S. Office of Education for failing—despite frequent pleas—to show sex differentials in faculty rank and pay when collecting and analyzing data in higher education. The need is great for "objective data to support what we know is flagrant discrimination against women in academia," AAUW representative Ruth M. Oltman told Editorial Research Reports. The President's task force had made a similar recommendation. In the course of a recent survey, the association itself uncovered several hundred case histories of sex discrimination in higher education and hundreds more of job discrimination against educated women.

Women are ignoring St. Paul's admonition that they "keep silence in the churches." They are demanding—and to some degree, getting—their "rights" in leading American religious groups. Women delegates warned the American Baptist Convention in May 1970 that they would demand a woman be named president at the following year's meeting. The National Council of Churches in December 1969 chose its first woman president, Cynthia Wedel. The Lutheran Church in America yielded to feminist pressure by changing its bylaws on June 29, 1970, to permit women to become ordained ministers. Approximately one-fourth of the 235 member churches of the World Council of Churches ordain women. Some orders of Roman Catholic nuns have adopted secular practices to avoid submission to the church's "male mystique."[8] Perhaps most extraordinary of all, a girl is studying to become a rabbi at a Hebrew seminary in Cincinnati.

Support for Proposed 'Equal Rights' Amendment

Another sign of the new wave of feminist militancy is the revival of support for an "Equal Rights" amendment to the Constitution. The proposed amendment, stating simply that "Equality of rights under the law shall not be denied or abridged by the United States or by any state on account of sex," has been introduced in every session of Congress since 1923. Backers of the amendment have never been able to win congressional approval so that it could be presented to the various state legislatures for ratification.

But in 1970 there was a new basis for hope. Rep. Martha W. Griffiths (D Mich.) extricated the proposal from the House Judiciary Committee, a burial ground for the measure in years past, by getting the required 218 signatures of members on a discharge petition. Once this was done the measure was scheduled for floor action, expected about Aug. 10. In the Senate, the proposal received its first hearings in 14 years and afterward won approval of the Constitutional Amendments Subcommittee. The subcommittee chairman, Birch Bayh (D Ind.), one of 82 senators sponsoring the proposal, predicted approval by the parent Senate Judiciary Committee and then floor action later in the session.

At least a dozen bills pending in Congress in August 1970 were aimed specifically at removing some form of discrimination against women. Rep. Edith Green (D Ore.) introduced a measure to (1) prohibit sex discrimination in any program

---

[8] See Joseph H. Fichter, "Holy Father Church," *Commonweal*, May 15, 1970, p. 216.

receiving federal financial assistance, (2) extend coverage of the Equal Pay Act of 1963 to executive, administrative and professional employees, and (3) extend the jurisdiction of the Civil Rights Commission to include cases of sex discrimination. Hearings on her proposals were held June 16-19. Another measure would, if passed, strengthen the enforcement powers of the Equal Employment Opportunity Commission, and extend coverage of the Civil Rights Act to include sex discrimination in academic and professional employment. Other measures would remedy inequities that working wives suffer under the Social Security Act, provide day care facilities for children of working women, and equalize treatment of married women and married men in the federal service in regard to housing and other benefits overseas and to survivorship benefits. These proposals for legislation also follow recommendations of the President's Task Force on the Rights and Responsibilities of Women.

All told, the women's rights movement appears to be moving ahead, especially on the job front. Sonia Pressman, a senior lawyer for the Equal Employment Opportunity Commission, told a meeting of labor relations officials in Boston, April 29, 1970: "What we have seen in the past five years is nothing short of a revolution—a revolution in the legal rights of women to equality on the job and a revolution in the expectations of women with regard to such equality." However, she added: "There has not yet been a corresponding revolution in the employment status of women—in the jobs they hold and the salaries they earn."

Women in Employment, Education, Politics

THE STRONGEST drive for sex equality comes from working women. Entry into the labor force puts a hard dollars-and-cents value on equal rights. This is true of nearly all women who work, whether in factories, in offices, or in the professions. The continuing growth of the female labor force, especially the recent spurt upward, has therefore been a great stimulus to the women's rights movement. Nearly 31 million American women worked in early 1970, accounting for two-fifths of the entire labor force. Working women composed 42 per cent of all women 16 or older, in contrast to 23 per cent (8.2 million) half a century earlier.

Equally significant is the rising percentage of wives and mothers who work. The typical working woman in 1920 was single; if she married she quit work for good unless widowhood or desertion left her with no other means of support. The current pattern for a woman who marries is to remain employed, quitting only a few years for child-bearing and child-rearing. Two-fifths of all married women are in the labor force today compared with one-fourth in the mid-1950s. Wives accounted for 30 per cent of all working women in 1949 but 60 per cent in 1970.[9] An acceleration of the working-wife trend in recent years is due largely to younger women. The portion of wives under 35 in the labor market rose from 28 to 40 per cent during the past decade, with the steepest increases occurring in 1968-69.[10] One-third of all women with children of pre-school age were working or seeking work in 1969, almost twice as many as nine years earlier. Among mothers whose children had reached school age, almost one-half of them were working.

Although feminism is strongest among working women, the much-reported discontent among young housewives adds another spur to the equalization movement. This discontent is manifested mainly among college-educated young women who find routine homemaking tasks dull and damaging to the image of themselves acquired during their college days. The relatively high level of female education in the United States thus contributes to the many forces pressing on women to seek a fuller life beyond the sphere of domesticity.

The great growth in higher education of women occurred during the early decades of this century. The proportion of women earning college degrees fell during the 1940s, to pick up sharply in the 1950s for bachelor degrees but much more slowly for advanced degrees. As of March 1968 some 4.5 million women above age 25 had completed at least four years of college. The figure was sure to grow rapidly. Another study showed that one-fifth of all 21-year-old women were college graduates.[11]

---

[9] Elizabeth Waldman, "Changes in the Labor Force Activities of Women," *Monthly Labor Review*, June 1970, p. 11. A higher portion of Negro wives work than white wives but the gap is narrowing. As of March 1969, 51 per cent of Negro wives and 39 per cent of white wives were in the labor force.

[10] In the 12-month period that ended in March 1969, the total working population grew by 1.8 million and working wives accounted for 43 per cent of that increase. Among these 775,000 wives, 300,000 were ages 20-24. The baby boom after World War II only partly explains why women in this age group are so numerous in the work force. Their portion of the population rose by one-third between 1960 and 1969 but their participation in the labor force more than doubled.

[11] Department of Labor, *Trends in Educational Attainment of Women*, October 1969, pp. 5, 12.

The more education a woman has, the more likely she is to be engaged in paid employment, regardless of her marital status. The following table shows the relationship:

Education	Employed
5 years college or more	71 per cent
4 years college	54 per cent
High school graduation	48 per cent
Less than 8 years schooling	24 per cent

A Department of Labor study for the years 1952-68 showed exceptionally high employment for highly educated women in the 20-24 and 45-54 age groups. Particularly significant, however, was that among women college graduates the greatest increase in labor force participation came from the 25-34 age group. This is normally a period women shun outside jobs because of small children in the family.

Women's Work: Lower Paid and Less Prestigious

Labor force participation does not tell the whole story of woman's status in employment. Though most of the legal barriers to equality of opportunity in the work world have fallen away, the over-all picture for the woman worker has not changed very much in the half-century since women got the vote. Women still get the poorest paying, least prestigious jobs;[12] they are still scarce in the professions except for traditional and relatively low-paid careers in nursing, school teaching, and social work; and they have not captured more than a handful of commanding positions in business, education or other fields. Moreover, women workers are unemployed more often than men.[13]

Male-female pay differences run the occupational scales from top to bottom, just as they did a half-century ago. On a percentage basis, women's pay has fallen further behind men's in recent years, as the following Department of Labor statistics illustrate.

Year	Women	Men	Salary income as % of men's
1955	$2,719	$4,252	63.9
1960	3,293	5,417	60.8
1965	3,823	6,375	60.0
1968	4,457	7,664	58.2

---

[12] "No matter what sphere of work women are hired for or select, like sediment in a wine bottle they seem to settle to the bottom."—Cynthia Fuchs Epstein, *Woman's Place* (1970), p. 2. See "Women's Place in the Economy," *E.R.R.*, 1957 Vol. I, p. 8.

[13] Unemployment rates in 1969 averaged 2.8 per cent for men and 4.9 per cent for women. Unemployment rates for white women were more favorable, however, than for non-white men. Figures for 1969 were 2.5 per cent for white males; 3.8 per cent for white females; 4.3 per cent for non-white males and 5.8 per cent for non-white females.

The pay gap varies by occupation. But even where it is smallest, in the professional-technical worker and sales worker categories, a woman's earnings are only about two-thirds as high as a man's. Among other workers the gap widens, to the point that women sales workers earn less than one-half what their male counterparts do. (See table, opposite page.) Another measure of the gap in the earnings of women and men who work full-time the year-round is shown in the following table of wage-salary income distribution for the year 1968.

Earnings	Women	Men	Earnings	Women	Men
	(in percentages)			(in percentages)	
Less than $3,000	20.0	7.5	$7,000 to $10,000	10.9	30.9
$3,000 to $5,000	40.0	12.6	$10,000 to $15,000	2.5	19.5
$5,000 to $7,000	26.0	23.1	$15,000 and over	0.4	8.2

There is no indication that the trend has been reversed since 1968 when the foregoing statistics were gathered. A study of expected salaries for June 1970 college graduates indicated that women entering upon careers in accounting, chemistry, economics, engineering, liberal arts and mathematics could expect to earn anywhere from $86 to $18 less per month than male graduates.[14] The inability of women to move up the managerial and professional ladders, even when they are qualified to do so, accounts in part for their relatively low pay. The Equal Employment Opportunity Commission released statistics in 1969 indicating that women and nonwhite males were often engaged in work far below their abilities and educational qualifications. Another survey involving 150 business companies showed that only one in ten had as many as 5 per cent of its managerial positions filled with women. Four companies in ten had no women in the higher ranks of management.[15]

Meager Female Representation in the Professions

American women comprise only seven per cent of the nation's physicians,[16] four per cent of its architects, three per

---

[14] Frank S. Endicott, *Trends in Employment and University Graduates in Business and in Industry* (publication of Northeastern University, 1970).

[15] American Society for Personnel Administration-Bureau of National Affairs, *ASPA-BNA Survey: Employment of Women* (1970).

[16] Of 29 countries reporting to the Medical Women's International Association recently, the United States ranked 26th in the percentage of doctors who are women. Only Madagascar, Spain and South Viet Nam ranked lower. Women comprised 25 per cent of the doctors in Finland, Israel, and the Philippines; 20 per cent in Germany, 16 per cent in England, 13 per cent in France.

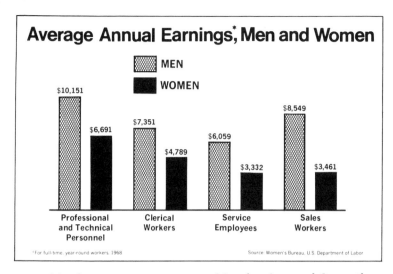

Average Annual Earnings,* Men and Women

MEN
WOMEN

$10,151		$7,351				$8,549	
	$6,691			$6,059			
			$4,789				
					$3,332		$3,461

Professional and Technical Personnel | Clerical Workers | Service Employees | Sales Workers

*For full-time, year-round workers. 1968.

Source: Women's Bureau, U.S. Department of Labor

cent of its lawyers, two per cent of its dentists and fewer than one per cent of its engineers. Even in professions in which women predominate, they rarely rise to the top. Seventy per cent of all teachers are women but the higher one goes on the educational and pay scales, the scarcer women become. Only one-fifth of all college teachers are women and few of them are in prestigious institutions or hold high-ranking professorial posts.[17] Even in areas of education where women predominate, men are often found in top positions. Males often head women's colleges.[18] Nine out of ten elementary school teachers are women but only about two of every ten principals are women.[19]

Perhaps the greatest disappointment of the women's rights movement is that so few women have held public office. Mrs. Carrie Chapman Catt had warned her fellow suffragists on the eve of victory that winning the vote would not admit them to the inner sanctum of political power; a "locked door" would still bar their entry. "You will have a long hard fight before you get behind that door," she said, "...but if you really

---

[17] The University of Chicago faculty, in the spring of 1969, included only 81 women among its 1,179 members. Only 11 of 476 full professors were women. These ratios "compare favorably...with those universities which...view themselves as 'elite'."—University of Chicago Committee on Women.

[18] Men hold presidencies of Bryn Mawr, Mount Holyoke, Sarah Lawrence and Vassar. A tendency to appoint men presidents of prestigious women's colleges may be related to moves to convert them to co-educational institutions.

[19] Report on sampling of 365 members of the National Education Association's Department of Elementary School Principals, *The National Elementary Principal*, November 1969, p. 81. See also Department of Labor, *1969 Handbook on Women Workers*, p. 97.

want women's vote to count, make your way there."[20] Few
women have made it behind that locked door; in partisan
politics, the pattern of male chairman and female vice-
chairman prevails almost universally.[21]

Diminishing Number of Women in Elective Posts

As for winning elective office, women have actually back-
slid. Only 11 women—six Democrats and five Republicans—
were among the 535 members of Congress in 1970, eight
fewer than in 1961-62 when their numbers reached an all-
time high of 19. In the entire 54-year period since Rep. Jean-
nette Rankin (R Mont.) became the first woman to be elected
to Congress[22] in 1916, only 75 women have served in the
federal legislature. Only 10 of them have been senators. One
of these, Sen. Margaret Chase Smith (R Maine), now in her
fourth term, is unique for having made political office a lifetime career and having attained recognition as one of the
more able and influential members of the Senate.[23] Her
nearest rival in effectiveness, Mrs. Maurine B. Neuberger (D
Ore.), was elected to the Senate in 1960 after having served
three terms in the state legislature. She did not stand for re-
election in 1966. The route to the Senate for all 10 led through
widowhood, each having been appointed or elected to fill the
term of a deceased husband. Seven of the ten served only a
few months or less. Sen. Hattie Caraway (D Ark.), appointed
in 1931 and re-elected until defeated in 1944, was a passive
figure in the Senate, though through seniority she became
chairman of a minor committee.[24]

Among the 66 women who have served in the House of Representatives, only a few have wielded significant power in that
body. Prominent among them were Edith Nourse Rogers (R

---

[20] Address before League of Women Voters' first congress, Chicago, Feb. 14, 1920,
cited by Eleanor Flexner, *Century of Struggle: The Woman's Rights Movement in the
United States* (1959), p. 326.

[21] Edward J. Flynn, former Democratic National Chairman, described the ideal national committeewoman: "She must be handsome, a lady, able to introduce the President gracefully, and wear orchids well; she must have an acceptable bank account—and
she must never, never interfere with party policy."—Quoted by Barbara Wendell Kerr,
"Don't Kid the Women," *Woman's Home Companion*, October 1956, p. 4.

[22] Miss Rankin served two widely separated single terms—in 1917-18 and again in
1941-42. In each term she cast a lonely vote against a declaration of war. In recent
years Miss Rankin has given public support to women's peace movements. See CQ
Weekly Report, July 10, 1970, pp. 1745-1748.

[23] Mrs. Smith was a member of the Republican State Committee in Maine (1930-
36), secretary to Rep. Clyde H. Smith (R Maine) whom she married, congresswoman
1940-48, and senator, 1949 to the present.

[24] Mrs. Caraway "seldom spoke on the Senate floor, preferring to do crossword
puzzles during debate....[She] frequently made the statement that she always voted the
way 'Thad' [her deceased husband, Sen. Thaddeus Caraway] would have voted."—
Martin Gruber, *Women in American Politics: An Assessment and Sourcebook* (1968),
p. 124.

WOMEN MEMBERS OF CONGRESS

Years	Senate	House	Years	Senate	House
1947-48	0	8	1959-60	1	16
1949-50	1	9	1961-62	2	17
1951-52	1	10	1963-64	2	11
1953-54	2	11	1965-66	2	10
1955-56	1	16	1967-68	1	11
1957-58	1	15	1969-70	1	10

Mass.), who served 18 terms (1925-60), Mary T. Norton (D N.J.), 13 terms (1925-50), and Frances Payne Bolton (R Ohio), 14 terms (1941-68). The 10 congresswomen now in office are highly regarded as effective and independent-minded legislators. Most of them have displayed strong staying powers. The only first-termer is the first Negro woman to serve in Congress, Shirley Chisholm of Brooklyn, who has said "in the political world I have been far oftener discriminated against because I am a woman than because I am black."[25]

The women's division of the Republican National Committee counted 306 women of both major parties serving in state legislatures in 1970, about 40 fewer than 10 years earlier. The 306 are spread over the legislatures of 49 states; only New Hampshire has a sizable number (62). Larger urbanized states, particularly, have few women legislators. New York has four, California three and New Jersey one.

The prospect of a woman President is as remote as ever[26] and that of a woman governor serving in her own right almost as inconceivable. Of the three women who actually have been elected governor, all served as shadows of their husbands. Nellie Tayloe Ross, a Democrat, was elected governor of Wyoming in 1924 to fill out two years of her deceased husband's term but was defeated in 1926 for re-election. James E. Ferguson, who had been impeached and removed as governor of Texas in 1917, successfully campaigned in 1924 for the election of his wife, using the slogan "Two governors for the price of one." Mrs. Miriam A. ("Ma") Ferguson was defeated in 1928, but re-elected in 1932, with her husband again serving as mentor. Lurleen Wallace was elected governor of

[25] See *CQ Weekly Report*, July 10, 1970, pp. 1745-48. Other congresswomen today are Leonor K. Sullivan (D Mo.), Edith Green (D Ore.), Martha W. Griffiths (D Mich.), Florence P. Dwyer (R N.J.), Julia B. Hansen (D Wash.), Catherine May (R Wash.), Patsy T. Mink (D Hawaii), Charlotte T. Reid (R Ill.), and Margaret M. Heckler (R Mass.).

[26] Three women received one or more votes for the presidential nomination at the 1924 Democratic convention. Nellie Tayloe Ross received 31 votes on the first ballot in 1928 for the Democratic vice-presidential nomination. Sen. Margaret Chase Smith received 30 votes in 1964 for the Republican presidential nomination.

Alabama in 1966 as a sit-in for her husband, George A. Wallace, who was constitutionally barred from succeeding himself.[27]

Only 31 women hold state elective positions outside the legislatures, a drop from 41 a decade earlier. Five are secretaries of state, 11 are state treasurers, two are state supreme court justices.[28] The meager showing in elective office is matched by lists of women appointees. In its publication *Women in Public Service*, the Republican National Committee listed 309 women appointed to "key positions in the federal government, in international affairs, and on important committees and commissions" in the first 16 months of the Nixon administration. Thirty-five of the posts were described as "high-level, policy-making positions." These positions, however, tended to be concerned with what are regarded as traditional women's interests. Another list of 273 women in federal service, offered as a sampling of "the type of positions women have achieved," included two ambassadors (Carol Laise to Nepal and Eileen R. Donovan to Barbados), an Assistant Secretary of Health, Education and Welfare (Patricia Hitt) and six members of U.S. missions to the United Nations.

Women's organizations long have pushed for more appointments of women to governmental posts. The National Federation of Business and Professional Women's Clubs maintains a "talent bank"—a roster of names and biographies of exceptionally qualified women—which it regularly submits to the White House. The federation and other organizations concerned with women's status are particularly concerned that there is no woman member of the President's cabinet and that no woman has ever been appointed to the Supreme Court.[29]

Male prejudice against women in high office, usually kept politely under cover, came to the surface when Rep. Patsy T. Mink (D Hawaii), at a meeting of the Democrats' Committee on National Priorities, April 30, 1970, urged that women's

---

[27] Mrs. Wallace died in office in May 1968. Wallace, now seeking re-election himself, won the Democratic nomination in June 1970 and is without a Republican opponent in November.

[28] The states with women in these elective offices are Alabama, Arkansas, Arizona, California, Colorado, Connecticut, Idaho, Kansas, Kentucky, Louisiana, Mississippi, New Mexico, North Dakota, North Carolina, Pennsylvania, South Dakota and Wyoming.

[29] The only two women cabinet officers were Secretary of Labor Frances Perkins in the Franklin D. Roosevelt administration, and Secretary of Health, Education and Welfare Oveta Culp Hobby in the Eisenhower administration. Eight women today are judges of federal courts. Of the nation's entire roster of 8,750 judges, 300 are women, most of whom serve on county courts.

rights be given high priority. Mrs. Mink was challenged by a member of the committee, Dr. Edgar F. Berman, an ex-surgeon and close friend of former Vice President Hubert H. Humphrey. Dr. Berman contended that women were disqualified for jobs requiring important decisions because their menstrual cycle and menopause subjected them to "raging hormonal influences." A furor ensued when his remarks were divulged publicly some three months later and he was prompted to resign from the committee.

Issues and Portents for Equal Rights

FEMINIST LEADERS ponder today why feminism failed. Some say it is because women relaxed once they got the vote. Others say it is because the feminist movement became too narrowly concentrated on suffrage and lost connection with its revolutionary origins. "In many ways [the suffrage movement] was the red herring of the revolution—a wasteful drain on the energy of 70 years," writes Kate Millett, leading theorist of the women's lib. "Because the opposition was so monolithic and unrelenting, the struggle so long and bitter, the vote took on a disproportionate importance. And when the ballot was won, the feminist movement collapsed."[30] Women divided their support between the two major parties pretty much as men did. Some did not even bother to vote and women candidates could not count on the support of those who did. Once suffrage was won, no feminist issue carried much political weight.

The situation is not entirely different now. The percentage of women who vote has increased until it has nearly reached that of men.[31] Because of the higher portion of women in the voter-age population (53.3 per cent), women voters in 1968 actually outnumbered men (40 million to 38 million). Yet feminism is not a major political issue, though some persons in the women's rights movement predict that it will enter into the 1972 election.

---

[30] Kate Millett, *Sexual Politics* (1970), p. 83.

[31] In 1924, only one-third of the women but two-thirds of the men voted in national elections. In November 1968, 66 per cent of the women and 69.8 per cent of the men voted —U.S. Census Bureau, "Voting and Registration in the Election of November 1968" (Population Characteristics, Series P-20), pp. 10-11.

The battle to win the vote had been a heroic one. Over the half-century between the first introduction of the suffrage amendment in Congress in 1866 and final victory, the suffragists had conducted 480 campaigns to get legislatures to submit suffrage amendments to voters; 47 campaigns to get state constitutional conventions to write woman's suffrage into state constitutions; 277 campaigns to get state party conventions to include woman's suffrage planks; 30 campaigns to get national party conventions to adopt woman's suffrage planks in party platforms; and 19 campaigns with 19 successive Congresses.[32]

Suffragists suffered pain, contumely and arrest; they were the butt of jokes and insults. The unattractive image of the battle-axe feminist, devoid of feminine charm, rejected by men, and even a bit off her rocker—an image created by publicists for the opposition—is a heritage which still taints the feminist movement and makes many secretly sympathetic women leery of the label. Prominent among the anti-suffrage interests was the liquor industry, which had reason to fear women prohibitionists in the era of the corner saloon.[33]

In the end the doughty crusaders had no effective program for women's rights beyond suffrage. This was not true in the beginning. Pioneer feminists of the early 19th century had begun what then seemed an almost hopeless battle against an entrenched way of life, solidified by law, moral conviction, and religion, which kept women and especially married women in the status of chattels or at best dependent children. The early movement was by no means confined to a struggle for suffrage. More immediate concerns were control of property, of earnings, guardianship, divorce, opportunity for education and employment, lack of legal status, and the concept of female inferiority perpetuated by established religion.

The Woman's Rights Convention at Seneca Falls, N.Y., in July 1848 is generally cited as the beginning of the woman's suffrage movement in the United States. But the Declaration of Principles which Mrs. Elizabeth Cady Stanton read at that meeting and which thereafter became a sacred text of the movement, was a much broader and more revolutionary document than a simple claim for the franchise. Paraphrasing the

---

[32] Carrie Chapman Catt's tally, cited by Eleanor Flexner, *Century of Struggle: The Woman's Rights Movement in the United States* (1969), p. 173.

[33] Suffrage has been unfairly blamed for prohibition, however. Women had not received the vote nationwide when the 18th Amendment (prohibition) became effective in early 1920. At that time they could cast a ballot only in the individual states that had already granted them the franchise.

Declaration of Independence, it held "these truths to be self-evident: that all men and women are created equal." It itemized woman's grievances—"a history of repeated injuries and ursurpations on the part of man toward woman"—and pledged an unremitting fight, in the face of anticipated punishment from society, to attain the goal of equality. The meeting adopted a number of resolutions, unanimously except for one —a call for woman suffrage, which carried by a small margin.

Attempt to Link Women's Cause With Negroes'

Today's new breed of feminists tends to equate the role of women with that of the black—an analogy irritating to many blacks—and to link their cause with that of the racial minorities as a struggle against the dominance of the white man in American society. The linkage has a historical precedent in the close association of women's rights and the anti-slavery movement beginning in the 1830s. "The first conscious feminists," Eleanor Flexner wrote, were women who learned in the fight to free the slaves how to fight for their own rights.

It was in the abolition movement that women first learned to organize, to hold public meetings, to conduct petition campaigns. As abolitionists they first won the right to speak in public and began to evolve a philosophy of their place in society and of their basic rights. For a quarter of a century the two movements, to free the slave and liberate the woman, nourished and strengthened one another.

It was the sharpest of disappointments that the 14th Amendment—and then the 15th—failed to include women in the extension of citizenship rights to Negroes. "Many of the early suffragists never recovered from their humiliating discovery that Negro men were considered better qualified to vote than they. In consequence, it became customary for them to exploit racial prejudices to their own advantage."[34]

The suffrage cause became more and more marked by the prejudices of upper-middle-class women in the post-Civil War period. Negro women were segregated or discouraged from joining suffrage parades. Rather than argue against the degradation and exploitation of women, the suffragists offered woman suffrage as a means of putting down blacks and the foreign-born. In effect, they appealed for a restricted franchise that would give middle-class women the vote but deny it to the despised classes. Though the suffrage movement dropped this bid for support in the last decade of the struggle, it left

---

[34] William L. O'Neill, *Everyone Was Brave: The Rise and Fall of Feminism in America* (1969), p. 69.

among working women a residue of hostility toward the women's rights movement.

Division Over Goals: Equal Rights or Protection

This division was most concretely expressed in the post-suffrage debate over the proposed Equal Rights amendment. Women's organizations for years were sharply divided on the amendment. The National Woman's Party has been almost solely concerned with its adoption but the party has never had much rank-and-file appeal. The amendment's chief supporters over the years have been business and professional women, represented by the National Federation of Business and Professional Women's Clubs. On the other side were women in trade unions and in social reform organizations who believed it would be detrimental to the majority of working women and would throw out laws protecting married women and children. They fought instead for the array of social reform legislation—wage-hour laws, child labor bans, social security and welfare measures, provisions for maternal-child health and other public health programs.

On the question of equal rights, they have held that men and women should be treated equitably but not necessarily identically where their interests differ. The success in putting over this point of view in the post-suffrage years is indicated by the vast body of legislation and regulation protective of women—limiting hours, forbidding night work, setting minimum wages in low-paid, woman-dominated employment, and so forth. Only in recent years has support for this body of law, now falling away under the hammer of the Civil Rights Act, been declining. Two formidable organizations, the League of Women Voters and the American Association of University Women, dropped their opposition to the Equal Rights amendment some years ago.

The strongest opponent today is organized labor, a frequent target of feminists who regard it as just another male-dominated institution controlling the lives of women. Women compose 20 per cent of the total membership of labor unions but occupy virtually none of the leadership positions. Even unions with large female memberships, like those in the clothing trades, have always been headed by men.

A new breed of feminists is determined to give up the privileges as well as the penalties of lower-level status. It is in keeping with the current mood that the latest of a series of presidential study groups on the question of women's rights—

each President in recent years having felt the need to appease women with such a study—emphasizes "responsibilities" as well as the "rights" of women. The return to radical feminism is by no means confined to women of the guerrilla theater stamp. The vision of the "new woman" pressed by radical feminists has come within view of old-line women's organizations. An infusion of activist energy from black women and young women fresh off the campus has reached these relatively conservative strongholds of feminist power.

Dividing lines between the old and new brands of feminism may be disappearing. Mrs. Elizabeth Duncan Koontz, director of the Women's Bureau in the Department of Labor, has belittled the theory that the sexes have to be "highly distinct in their roles, polarized in their interests and abilities." She joined the new feminists in criticizing the education system, the news media, the advertising trade, and child-rearing dicta as conditioning women to accept a second-rung status, limited in range of activity. The influence of new feminism has also reached the Young Women's Christian Association, which issued a *Work Book* at its 1970 convention in Houston stating: "It is essential that women move beyond being sexual playthings of the male to an affirmation of their role as human beings, with capacity for leadership and contribution in varied ways....They need an identity of their own."

What this closing of the ranks will mean to the future status of women is not certain. The great majority of women give little evidence that they object to the status quo. The chief determinant of the future may be simply the need of the economy—and the individual family—for the earnings of the wife-and-mother. In the end it may be that the husband and wife will routinely share in both housework and family earnings. Now has proposed paternity as well as maternity leave for employees so that mothers can pursue careers and fathers can have more time with the children. Some men may even get to like it that way.

Human INTELLIGENCE

by

William Gerber

MEASUREMENT OF MAN'S MENTAL ABILITY
Dispute Over Bearing of Race on Intelligence
Supposed Cultural Bias in Intelligence Tests
Mental Attributes Constituting Intelligence
Two Sides of Mental Tests and Intelligence

GROWTH OF KNOWLEDGE ABOUT THE MIND
Evolution of Animal and Human Intelligence
Progress in Understanding of Mental Abilities
Development of the Various Intelligence Tests
Reaction Against Depersonalization of Testing

PROSPECT OF BROADENING MENTAL HORIZONS
Influence of Age and Environment on the I.Q.
Effects of Nutrition and Drugs on Intelligence
Importance of Home Environment and Schooling
Alliance Between the Brain and the Computer

1 9 6 9
Aug. 20

HUMAN INTELLIGENCE

L EADING THINKERS of the western world suggest that human intelligence is fated to save or destroy mankind, perhaps within a matter of decades. Britain's C. P. Snow is pessimistic about the prospects of turning the mind of man away from its bent for making the earth uninhabitable through pollution, overpopulation or the use of nuclear weapons. On this side of the Atlantic, Buckminster Fuller argues that man's chances of survival and well-being are not dimmed but brightened by new achievements of the human intellect.

The manned moon landing and the deciphering of the D.N.A. genetic code [1] are monuments to optimists among scientist-intellectuals. They contend that for the first time in history man has the ability to play a conscious, active role in his own evolution and that by tapping cosmic resources he may nullify the Malthus theory of the inevitability of famine. [2]

What determines human intelligence? Is it fixed and immutable at a child's birth, or does it change with time and circumstance? And if it does change, what circumstances can best foster its growth and development?

These questions once agitated only a small group of scholars and scientists, J. McVicker Hunt has noted. But no longer. "Today they have acquired urgent and social political significance. The fates of vast programs and many a career may hinge on the conclusions of the most recondite social-psychological study." [3] A scholarly paper on race and intelligence appearing in the Winter 1969 issue of the *Harvard Educational Review* made headlines, particularly in south-

---

[1] See "Genetics and the Life Process," *E.R.R.*, 1967 Vol. II, pp. 905-907.

[2] Thomas Robert Malthus, English economist and sociologist, propounded the theory, in *An Essay on the Principle of Population* in 1798, that world population was mathematically certain to outstrip the food supply because population increases by geometrical ratio while the means of subsistence expand only by arithmetical ratio.

[3] J. McVicker Hunt (chairman of White House Task Force on the Role of the Federal Government in Early Childhood and Education), "Black Genes—White Environment," *Trans-action*, June 1969, p. 12.

ern newspapers, and was used extensively by the defense in a Virginia school integration lawsuit. The paper brought to a boil a simmering dispute in the educational community over the relative value of heredity and environment in childhood learning.

Dispute Over Bearing of Race on Intelligence

"Compensatory education has been tried and it apparently has failed." In those words Arthur R. Jensen, professor of educational psychology at the University of California at Berkeley, opened the controversial article. He specifically attacked the theoretical basis of the Head Start program, and in effect the desegregation of schools generally, by saying that "No one has yet produced any evidence based on a properly controlled study to show that representative samples of Negro and white children can be equalized in intellectual ability through statistical control of environment and education."

In support of his thesis, Jensen asserted that I.Q. tests showing average scores of black people to be 15 points below those of white people constituted evidence that "genetic factors are strongly implicated in the average Negro-white intelligence difference." The idea that genetic factors— rather than environment—may be responsible for the lower I.Q. scores of Negro children is "anathema to many social scientists," Jensen acknowledged. He added that although many have denounced the idea, "it has been neither contradicted nor discredited by evidence."

Five scholars challenged Jensen's views in the spring issue of the *Harvard Educational Review*, and a prestigious group within the American Psychological Association—the Council of the Society for the Psychological Study of Social Issues —stated: "There are marked differences in intelligence test scores when one compares a random sample of whites and Negroes. What is equally clear is that little definitive evidence exists that leads to the conclusion that such differences are innate." [4]

C. P. Snow, on the other hand, said last spring that he was prepared to support the genetic school of thought—although he specifically refrained from commenting on the Jensen thesis. Lord Snow, a physicist and author, told a

---

[4] Statement published in *Trans-action*, June 1969, p. 6.

Jewish audience in New York, March 31, 1969, that the record of intellectual achievement among Jews was remarkable "quite outside any sort of statistical probabilities" and even after environmental factors were considered. "Is there something in the Jewish gene-pool that produces talent on quite a different scale from, say, the Anglo-Saxon gene-pool?" he asked. "I am prepared to believe that may be so."

Some behavioral scientists say the question of innate superiority may never be settled because racial stock has been diluted. Others say the question will be unanswerable until black, Puerto Rican and Indian children in America acquire the same educational opportunities and motivations as white children. Meanwhile, Winton H. Manning, executive director of research and development for the College Entrance Examination Board, has noted that mental tests, though aimed at "building a society based on merit and accomplishment rather than inherited privilege and social origins," appear to the underprivileged as "bulwarks of bias whose use denies equality of educational and job opportunity to Negroes and other minority groups disproportionately represented in the poverty population." [5]

Supposed Cultural Bias in Intelligence Tests

The Jensen controversy had its roots in earlier joustings between scholars who focused on the lower scores of Negroes in intelligence tests and scholars who stressed the element of cultural bias in the tests. The slum child, it was contended, might score poorly on intelligence tests because the tests reflect the dominant cultural patterns from which he is cut off. Hence, his native wit is not recorded.

Psychologists sought during the 1960s to devise intelligence tests free of cultural bias and not requiring verbal skills. A test deemed almost culture-free, administered a few years ago to infants between the ages of one month and 15 months, revealed no noticeable Negro-white differences in intelligence.[6] However, not all psychologists are convinced about the freedom of tests from bias. Richard de Neufville of the Massachusetts Institute of Technology and Caryl Conner of the U.S. Office of Education, for example, said

---

[5] Winton H. Manning, "The Measurement of Intellectual Capacity and Performance," *Journal of Negro Education*, Summer 1968, p. 258.

[6] Nancy Bayley, "Comparisons of Mental and Motor Test Scores for Ages 1-15 Months by Sex, Birth Order, Race, Geographical Location, and Education of Parents," *Child Development*, June 1965, p. 379.

the following year in a different context but without qualification: "There are *no* culture-free tests." [7]

William Shockley, who had shared the Nobel Prize for physics in 1956 as co-inventor of the transistor, asked the National Academy of Sciences to investigate the possible genetic origin of racial differences in intelligence, but the Academy in 1967, in 1968, and on April 29, 1969, voted to table his proposal on the ground that, in the words of the Academy's president. "It is essentially impossible to do good research in this field as long as there are such great social inequities."

A newspaper columnist commented that "The refusal of these eminent scientists to even look into the matter has a hollow ring. . . . Modern science didn't begin until men were willing to test the nature of materials. Is the National Academy of Sciences going back to alchemy?" [8]

Mental Attributes Constituting Intelligence

Reluctance of the National Academy of Sciences to undertake research on race and intelligence is presumably based not on fondness for alchemy but on hesitancy to step into a conceptual quagmire. The concept of race is lacking in precision and that of intelligence is murky. Some persons believe that intelligence is an integral attribute, not divisible into separate components; others believe that it is a complex of two, three, four or more elements. One authority some years ago despairingly defined intelligence as whatever it is that intelligence tests test.

Certain animals display attributes that have elements of intelligence. Two University of Nevada scientists, for example, have taught a young female chimpanzee to talk in the same kind of sign language used by the deaf. As reported by the *Washington Post* on Aug. 16, 1969, the young chimp knows at least 60 "words" and regularly uses them in spontaneous combinations much as a human baby might begin to combine words and ideas. The chimp will "say," in appropriate combinations of signs: "Go Out," while still some distance from a door; "Listen Dog," when she hears

---

[7] Richard de Neufville and Caryl Conner, "How Good Are Our Schools? Armed Forces Qualification Test Provides a Clue," *American Education*, October 1966, p. 3.

[8] Jenkin Lloyd Jones, "Genetics Turns Off the Scientists," *Washington Evening Star*, May 24, 1969, p. A4.

an unseen dog barking; "Open Key," asking for a key to open a locked door. This experiment could make scientists revise their whole idea of animal intelligence.

Some of those who consider that intelligence is a unitary attribute identify it as the ability to learn from experience. Scientists have collected an immense treasury of knowledge about the intelligence of mice, if not of men, since the ability of mice to learn useful procedures through the motivations of reward and punishment has been studied from many angles. Other authorities, while agreeing that intelligence is not a compound quality, say that it is essentially common sense, a characteristic possessed by different people in radically different magnitudes, but with which everyone feels that he himself has been endowed in goodly measure. Lightner Witmer, for many years director of the psychological clinic at the University of Pennsylvania, defined intelligence as the ability to solve a new problem.

John Dewey suggested that intelligence is composed of two elements: power to imagine a desirable future and power to invent means of realizing that future. Many psychologists regard intelligence as a combination of three kinds of aptitudes: abstract or linguistic, including deftness in the use of symbols, such as words, numbers, diagrams, formulas, and pictures; mechanical, including dexterity with tools and machinery; and social, including poise, tact, and insight. David Wechsler, author of mental tests widely used for children and adults, likewise holds that there are three basic components of intelligence, but he enumerates them as the ability to think rationally, to act purposefully, and to deal effectively with one's environment.

Investigators who reject the single, double, and triple views of intelligence feel that they must find room in the concept for abilities such as discernment, discrimination, memory, inductive and deductive capacity, understanding of relations between things which seem unrelated, creativity, and evaluative judgment. J. P. Guilford, author of *The Nature of Human Intelligence,* has constructed a model of intelligence in the form of a cube with 40 factors in each dimension. Of the total of 120 components of intelligence, he regards 80 as important. The popular Stanford-Binet test, he notes, covers only 28 of the 80 important factors.

Although no precise identification of intelligence, or classification of its components, has won general adoption, that fact does not mean that no progress has been made. Psychology as an experimental science is less than a century old, and the process of refining the concept of intelligence has had an even shorter history. Human intelligence is not always an unmixed blessing. Ecclesiastes, having probed the depths of wisdom (roughly coextensive with intelligence), reported:

> I gave my heart to know wisdom, and to know madness and folly: I perceived that this also is vexation of spirit.
>
> For in much wisdom is much grief: and he that increaseth knowledge increaseth sorrow.

A recent observer commented with similarly restrained enthusiasm on the uses of reason (another close correlate of intelligence): "Reason can fight crime or plan it; illuminate human behavior or seek to manipulate it; devise liberating theories of reform or oppressive theories of revolution." [9] Thus, homo sapiens can employ his intelligence constructively or destructively.

Growth of Knowledge About the Mind

LIFE, and the foundations of mind, began when complex globules of matter reacted to environmental changes not only mechanically but also adaptively. Long ages later, in the advance of functional differentiation, some cells specialized in reception, transmission, and interpretation of stimuli. This beginning of nerve and brain cells was followed by grouping of such cells for storage, recognition, and correlation of impressions and for choice of responses.

The brains of animals grew in size and complexity over thousands of generations, with accompanying improvements in perception, prudence, and skill. One mentally agile species, simians, in the course of time developed manual dexterity. Their anthropoid descendants, making use of this potential, evolved into homo faber, the animal that used his intelligence for making tools. A giant step was taken when

---

[9] Nigel Calder, "How Much Decision-Making Can We Leave to the Machine?" *New Statesman*, May 17, 1968, p. 647.

this adaptively probing animal developed language and thereby immensely increased his facility in formation and manipulation of concepts. Creative imagination capped the process, and homo sapiens was born.

From the beginning, man lived in the society of those who dwelt within walking distance. The invention of writing and the wheel, and the domestication of animals, enabled the human species to form larger units and to undertake venturesome projects requiring the cooperation of communities and provinces. According to the French anthropologist Louis Weber, the progress of man's intelligence in society has occurred in cycles. During paleolithic times, technological discoveries, such as flaked stone tools, predominated; in the mesolithic period, the symbolic and speculative were foremost; in ancient Egypt, technology again; in Greece, speculation; in the Middle Ages, practical arts; in the Renaissance and modern times, conceptual science; and, now beginning, an era of new technological wonders.

Progress in Understanding of Mental Abilities

Not only was Greek culture, as Weber noted, a milestone in man's intellectual march, but the Greeks themselves viewed intelligence as a priceless gift of the gods. Plato regarded intelligence as the special virtue of the highest part of the soul, namely, cognition. He designated courage and self-control as the virtues of the other parts of the soul—will and feeling. Justice, Plato said, prevails when intelligence is given its proper role in the state; that is, when philosophers are kings.

Intelligentia—the word was first used by Cicero—was associated by the Romans with connoisseurship, skill, and art. In the Middle Ages, the notion of distinct, compartmentalized faculties of the mind, of which intelligence was one, along with perception, memory, imagination, and others, became crystallized. Immanuel Kant, at the end of the 18th century, still adhered to faculty psychology, but questioning of it was already in process during his lifetime.

Clarity and precision in the understanding of intelligence were significantly advanced in the 19th century by continental and British investigators. Germans who furthered this objective included Gustav T. Fechner and Wilhelm Wundt, who share the honor of establishing psychology as an experimental discipline. A French scholar, Hippolyte-

Adolphe Taine, in his treatise *De l'Intelligence* in 1870, mustered the evidence for interaction of mental phenomena and thus delivered the coup de grâce to faculty psychology. In England, Sir Francis Galton, cousin of Charles Darwin, discovered truths about distribution of superior intelligence in the total population through a statistical study of geniuses.

In the present century, important progress in the understanding of mental abilities was made by Swiss and American psychologists, among others. Jean Piaget, of the University of Geneva, studied the kinds of intelligent thinking done by children at various ages regarding the world around them. He found that serious reasoning, as distinct from intuition, begins at about the age of 10. Edward L. Thorndike, of Columbia University, performed experiments on human and animal learning which led him to conclude that intelligence is multi-modal; for example, one who is excellent in learning vocabulary may be poor in learning arithmetic.

Development of the Various Intelligence Tests

Progress in understanding intelligence made it possible to evaluate scientifically and numerically an individual's level of intelligence. Testing of mental proficiency in less scientific ways has had a long history, going back at least to examinations for the civil service in China more than 3,000 years ago. Those examinations depended in part on rote learning, but they also called into play the candidates' ability to interpret literary and religious classics.

James McKeen Cattell, an American psychologist, apparently was the first to use the term mental tests, in an article "Mental Tests and Their Measurements" published in the British periodical *Mind* in 1890. Alfred Binet and his younger colleague, Théodore Simon, were commissioned in 1904 by Paris municipal authorities to devise tests for assessing the intelligence mainly of retarded children but also of children in general. The tests which they submitted, with norms for age groups, were published in 1905 and revised in 1908 and 1911. L. M. Terman and colleagues at Stanford University published American versions of the Binet-Simon tests in 1916 and later years.[10]

The U. S. Armed Forces have tested military personnel for mental ability since World War I. The results, made

---

[10] See "Educational Testing," *E.R.R.*, 1958 Vol. II, pp. 941-942.

available in the form of statistics for geographic, sex, age, racial, and other groupings, have been studied endlessly for clues to educational policy, national traits, and differences in the mental abilities of men and women, Caucasians and blacks, and other cross-sectionings. The tests now used by the Department of Defense cover vocabulary, arithmetic, spatial relationships, and mechanical ability. Both education and intelligence affect one's score in the tests. Military psychologists state explicitly that these are not intelligence tests.

The concept of the intelligence quotient [11] was introduced by Wilhelm Stern, an Austrian psychologist, in 1912, but its widespread use is credited to Terman. An important defect of the I.Q. test arises from the fact that ability to learn grows more slowly as age increases, whereas the I.Q. assumes, for example, that a child of ten normally has twice, and a child of fifteen three times, the intelligence of a child of five. To take account of the slowdown in growth of intelligence, Arthur S. Otis in 1922 developed the Index of Brightness, or Deviation I.Q., which is 100 plus or minus the subject's deviation from the norm for his age. [12]

The most popular intelligence tests in the United States today are the Stanford-Binet test, the Wechsler Intelligence Scales for Pre-School and School-Age Children, and the Wechsler Adult Intelligence Scale. The calculation of the I.Q. is generally made on the basis of a variation of the Otis deviation formula. Norms by which an individual's score can be compared with the national average are being steadily improved. Thus, the Stanford test of 1923 was standardized on the basis of a sample of 1,500 subjects, whereas the norms for the 1964 edition of the test were based on the test scores of some 800,000 children in all 50 states.

Reaction Against Depersonalization of Testing

The fervor with which the educational establishment attempted to gauge the intelligence of students and to classify them definitively on that basis led in some cases to excesses. There is, as noted by a professor of education and psychology at Michigan State University, "the danger that

---

[11] The highest mental age for which an individual can complete a test, divided by his chronological age, the result being multiplied by 100.

[12] For example, if the norm for a given age is 42 (that is, at that age the normal child gets 42 questions right out of 100), and the subject gets 35 right, then 35 minus 42 plus 100, or 93, is his score.

educational testing may place an indelible stamp of inferiority on a child, ruin his self-esteem and educational motivation, and determine his social status as an adult. . . . There
is some danger that we may forget our own inadequacies
and attempt to play God with the lives of other human
beings." [13] A professor at the California State College at
Hayward, discussing "misuses of testing and test results,"
complained that "Those who use tests have come to believe
in the test scores as a kind of absolute." [14]

The tendency to view test scores as absolute led to the
theory that students will learn better if they are grouped
homogeneously according to their test scores. [15] Ability
grouping on a large scale began around 1920 in the Detroit
high schools and spread rapidly, reaching a peak in the
1930s. Some school systems abandoned ability grouping
during the 1940s and 1950s, but a revival of the practice
occurred in the 1960s.

Marian Pope Franklin of the School of Education, University of North Carolina in Greensboro, has emphasized
that attainment of a score of 120 by two students in a
standard intelligence test does not mean that both scored
equally well in all the factors involved—memory, inductive
ability, deductive ability, verbal comprehension, the number
factor, the space factor, creativity, etc. It therefore may be
a mistake to assume that, if put in the same class, they will
make comparable progress in all school subjects. Prof.
Franklin, surveying research literature on ability, found
that "About half of the studies report students do better
when they are grouped homogeneously on ability and the
other half report they do better when grouped heterogen-
eously." [16]

Abuses of intelligence testing were recorded in a number
of books published in the early 1960s. [17] The educational
authorities of New York City informed the city's 800 public
school principals, Feb. 26, 1964, that group intelligence tests
would no longer be administered and that "an extensive

---

[13] Robert L. Ebel, "The Social Consequences of Educational Testing," in Anne
Anastasi (ed.), *Testing Problems in Perspective* (1966), pp. 21, 26-27.

[14] James R. Barclay, *Controversial Issues in Testing* (1968), p. 6.

[15] See "Schooling for Fast and Slow Learners," *E.R.R.*, 1955 Vol. II, pp. 809-827.

[16] Marian Pope Franklin, "Ability Grouping: The Research Is Inconclusive," in
Franklin (ed.), *School Organization; Theory and Practice* (1967), p. 424.

[17] Martin L. Gross, *The Brain Watchers* (1962); Banesh Hoffmann, *The Tyranny of
Testing* (1962); and Hillel Black, *They Shall Not Pass* (1963). Vance O. Packard in-
veighed against tests as an invasion of privacy in *The Naked Society* (1964).

achievement testing program" was being substituted. The notice to the principals stated that "Present group measures of intelligence provide an inadequate basis for judging the intellectual needs of children." Some teachers had tended to take the results of intelligence tests as a fixed measure of learning capacity. School systems in Los Angeles, St. Paul, and Washington, D. C., also have curtailed group I.Q. testing, and schools in Cleveland and Philadelphia are considering such a move, according to a survey reported in the *Wall Street Journal*, June 12, 1969.

Prospect of Broadening Mental Horizons

PSYCHOLOGISTS are moving away from the belief, once widely held, that intelligence is constant—that a child who has an I.Q. of 95 at age five will still have an I.Q. of 95, no more and no less, when he reaches the age of 15. If this were so, efforts to improve intelligence would be as pointless as efforts of a youth 5 feet 8 inches in height to become a six-footer.

There are now well-supported findings of psychologists that an individual's level of intelligence changes over time; that intelligence generally increases more rapidly in early than in later years; and that while minor changes in environment do not show up in intelligence test scores, major environmental changes result in marked differences in test scores. A professor of education at the University of Chicago, reporting the results of tests administered before and after major environmental changes, wrote:

> A conservative estimate of the effect of extreme environments on intelligence is about 20 I.Q. points. This could mean the difference between a life in an institution for the feeble-minded or a productive life in society. It could mean the difference between a professional career and an occupation which is at the semi-skilled or unskilled level.[18]

The same author also found evidence for rejecting the view that intelligence stops growing in the late teens. Intelligence, he said, apparently increases slowly after adolescence to about the age of 50.

---

[18] Benjamin S. Bloom, *Stability and Change in Human Characteristics* (1964), p. 89.

If intelligence is not fixed, and can be improved, it is important to know what measures will increase intelligence. In any case, it is premature to expect dramatic results. The factor of cultural lag will probably delay large-scale application of scientific findings in this field even when those findings attain a higher degree of confirmation than has been reached thus far.

Effects of Nutrition and Drugs on Intelligence

Measures that seem capable of affecting intelligence favorably are of two kinds: physiological and environmental. Physiological measures conducive to heightened intelligence include being born of bright parents, that is, inheritance of talent genes; administration by physicians or technicians of the right amount of oxygen in obstetrical work before and at the time of birth; improvement in nutrition, where it has been deficient; and taking of certain drugs. So far as inheritance, or eugenics, is concerned, one science writer, warning against expectation of miracles from this source alone, noted that "Biologists in 1969 talk of creating a crop of Einsteins with changes in genetic material, as though Einstein's experiences had nothing to do with the talent that emerged." [19]

Lack of proper nutrition was found to inhibit development of intelligence, in studies conducted by Myron Winick, associate professor of pediatrics at Cornell University's Medical College. Winick told participants in a Nutrition Institute at Cornell in July 1968 that babies who had suffered from malnutrition before and shortly after birth showed irreversible stunting of brain growth. Another expert reported a few months later that "Young children suffering from malnutrition from the age of four months to four years when tested at ages 7 to 14 years had I.Q.s at least 27 per cent lower than [the healthy children used as] controls." [20] By taking steps to eliminate or reduce hunger, society can help to prevent subnormal intelligence. But scientists do not yet know how to make an average person brilliant through food intake.

The same appears to be true regarding the effect of oxygen and drugs on intelligence; that is, scientists have learned only how to avoid and in some cases remedy intellectual sub-

---

[19] Patricia McBroom, "Nurture Key to I.Q.," *Science News*, March 8, 1969, p. 243.
[20] Lewis Jacobs, M.D., "Human Intelligence; The Physiological View," *Science Teacher*, September 1968, p. 16.

normality by these means but not to raise the intelligence level of normal brains. When children who had suffered from anoxia (lack of oxygen) at birth scored significantly lower in I.Q. tests at age three than did other children, obstetricians began devoting increased care to administration of oxygen to mother and child, with good results. In many cases, subnormal mental functioning due to hypothyroidism has responded dramatically to administration of thyroid preparations. David Kreck, professor of psychology at the University of California at Berkeley, has reported progress in improving the intelligence of subnormal animals through administration of glutamic acid and other drugs: "A class of chemicals has been isolated that can . . . raise a hereditarily stupid animal up to the performance of brighter animals of the same species." [21]

As to efforts to expand the intelligence of normal minds, the drug amphetamine, taken by students in "pep pills" to improve their grades in examinations, has been shown by controlled tests to enhance performance in a limited sphere, mainly grasp of spatial relations. No pill exists as yet that will improve reason or creativity or make man more responsive to reason. Medical science in the years immediately ahead will probably produce improved physiological means of raising low intelligence to normal levels. The human race will probably have to wait longer for chemical or biological devices capable of bestowing reason and superior wisdom.

Importance of Home Environment and Schooling

For physiological improvement of intelligence, available know-how is meager. But for environmental changes which may result in improved intelligence, or at least improved performance in intelligence tests, there are many prescriptions. The prescriptions are based on the fact that performance, whether in taking tests or in ordinary life situations, depends not only on native ability but also on a variety of environmental factors. Among these are quality of early schooling, cultural background, emotional stability, confidence and motivation.[22]

The National Institute of Mental Health, a bureau of the U. S. Public Health Service, conducted a two-year experiment involving the impact of environment on test scores.

[21] Quoted in the (London) *Times Educational Supplement,* June 28, 1968, p. 2123.
[22] See "Education of Slum Children," *E.R.R.,* 1964 Vol. II, pp. 785-788.

The experiment and the results were reported recently as follows:

> Psychologist Barl S. Schaefer sent tutors into the homes of 30 children living in a Washington ghetto. For two years, an hour a day, five days a week, the tutors carried in puzzles, toys and picture books. They played with the children, talked to them and took them on trips. At the end of two years, the 30 children, then three years old, had a mean I.Q. of 106. By contrast, a group of 30 similar children who were not helped had mean scores of 89.[23]

Less encouraging results were indicated by a recent study of Head Start—the federal program whose purpose is to improve the cultural background of underprivileged preschool children. The group of scholars who studied Head Start in 1968 and 1969 concluded in a preliminary report last April that children who participated in the program showed statistically insignificant differences "in their intellectual and socio-personal development from comparable children who did not attend." Robert H. Finch, Secretary of the Department of Health, Education and Welfare, to which the Head Start program was recently transferred from the Office of Economic Opportunity, on April 24 criticized the basis of the report as "not broad enough" and said that "Some people in our department feel the data was sloppy."

In the South San Francisco Unified School District, investigators studied the effect of teacher expectation on children's ability levels. They chose a group of pupils at random from each class and then intimated to the teacher that those pupils showed exceptional promise. They scored higher when tested later. "When teachers expected that certain children would show greater intellectual development, those children did show greater intellectual development." [24] The two investigators who conducted the study commented: "There may be here the makings of a benign cycle. Teachers may not only get more when they expect more; they may also come to expect more when they get more." [25]

Besides improved nutrition, drugs, environment, and schooling, there is another avenue to expansion of intelli-

---

[23] Patricia McBroom, *op. cit.*, p. 244.

[24] Robert Rosenthal (Harvard University) and Lenore Jacobson (San Francisco school system), "Self-Fulfilling Prophecies in the Classroom," in Martin Deutsch, Irwin Katz, and Arthur Jensen (eds.), *Social Class, Race and Psychological Development* (1968), p. 246.

[25] Robert Rosenthal and Lenore Jacobson, *Pygmalion in the Classroom; Teacher Expectation and Pupils' Intellectual Development* (1968), p. 178.

ence: construction and use of machines which can serve as an adjunct to the mind. The oldest device of this kind, the abacus, was used in China as early as the sixth century B.C. A noteworthy further step along this road was taken by Raymond Lull, a medieval logician who developed a series of rotating circles by which the conclusions derivable from various combinations of premises were mechanically exhibited. Blaise Pascal in 1642 invented an adding machine in which numerals were represented by positions of toothed wheels.

Alliance Between the Brain and the Computer

In recent years inventors, scholars, and cash register companies, mainly American, have produced better and better machines to perform arithmetical and logical operations. The first large-scale automatic computer, capable of receiving complex data and applying pre-set processes to them speedily, was built in 1944 by the International Business Machines Corporation. By now, about 40,000 computers are in use throughout the world.

Technicians who were engaged in improving the capabilities of computers developed methods by which a computer could appropriate new information mechanically, feed back the new information, and correct or change its operations on the basis of the new information. This led to the notion, not yet fully accepted, that a computer can "learn" and can properly be described as functioning through artificial intelligence. Those who object to calling a machine intelligent point out, for example, that computer vocabulary is limited to two words, yes and no. They observe also that computers operate in simple-minded ways such as multiplying one large number by another by adding the first figure to itself over and over until the required number of times has been reached.

Kenneth M. Sayre, of the University of Notre Dame, has said: "We simply do not understand the basis of *human* intelligence behavior well enough to argue definitively either for or against the possibility of machine intelligence." [26] Nigel Calder nevertheless predicts: "From present tentative beginnings, machine intelligence will certainly develop. Whether 10 years or 100 years elapse before machines are,

---

[26] Kenneth M. Sayre, "Intelligence, Bodies and Digital Computers," *Review of Metaphysics*, June 1968, p. 723.

by a wide range of objective tests, more intelligent than man, that day will surely come." [27]

The human who is bothered by this prospect can meanwhile take comfort in the experience of the Apollo 11 astronauts. They were guided unerringly to the moon by computer controls in their spacecraft. But in the final seconds before the first manned landing on the moon, astronauts Neil A. Armstrong and Edwin E. Aldrin Jr. discovered that their computer-directed lunar module was descending upon a crater filled with enormous boulders. The computer could not make a judgment—only the brain could. Armstrong took over the controls and flew the craft to a better landing site nearby.

---

[27] Nigel Calder, *op. cit.*, p. 646.

▼▼▼

Sexual Revolution: Myth or Reality

by

Richard L. Worsnop

SEXUAL REVOLUTION: MYTH OR REALITY

AMERICANS, the mass media proclaim, are front-line troops in a sexual revolution. Evidence of the upheaval is everywhere to be seen—in displays of nudity and simulated intercourse on stage and screen, in the reported increase of pre- and extra-marital relations abetted by oral contraceptives, in sex education classes in public schools, in the increasing visibility and militance of homosexuals. The end product of the sexual revolution, its supporters say, will be a "new morality" freed of hypocrisy and fear and grounded in tolerance.

Some psychologists and sexual behaviorists take quite a different view. Rollo May, a professor of psychology at New York University, believes that the chaotic state of current sexual mores is indicative of "a new form of puritanism." It differs from the old form in that "the Victorian person sought to have love without falling into sex; the modern person seeks to have sex without falling into love." [1] Whether it be called revolution or puritanism, the new sexual freedom is embraced mainly by the young. Many older people are deeply disturbed and offended by it. They seem to fear that greater sexual freedom inevitably means promiscuity. The sexual revolution, numerous adults feel, is part and parcel of wider social unrest and they resist it for that reason.

Homosexuals, male and female, have begun openly to clamor for repeal of restrictive laws. And the champions of women's rights in employment and society have become more assertive. To women militants, the new sexual freedom seems a mixed blessing. On the one hand they feel free to assert their right to choose mates and to become "bachelor mothers" if they desire. At the same time they complain that now, more than ever before, women are becoming sexual "objects," to be regarded perhaps as house pets rather than as individual persons.

---

[1] Rollo May, *Love and Will* (1969), pp. 46-47.

103

The belief that sexual mores are changing is attributable in large part to the work of scientists engaged in sexual research. Until late in the 19th century, the literature on sex was confined primarily to the works of theologians, moralists, and poets. An early but isolated scientific study of the subject was Richard von Krafft-Ebing's *Psychopathia Sexualis,* published in 1886.[2] Then, around a decade later, Sigmund Freud began to expound his theories of the importance of subconscious sexual drives in the working of the human mind. While the findings of Freud and of such contemporaries as Havelock Ellis proved invaluable, they were based mainly on the study of sexually disturbed or aberrant persons.

Controversy about Studies of Human Sexuality

The publication in 1948 of the first so-called Kinsey Report represented a new departure in sexual research.[3] Kinsey and his colleagues "talked to the average Joe Smith who works on Main Street, to the normal and decent everyday person who lives next door . . . to determine who, what, when, where, and how often," although they seldom asked why. Kinsey's most important contribution may have been to make sexual research respectable. "Now one could ask who, what, and when, and one could even obtain government funds and foundation grants. Suddenly, scientific journals offered to print reports, and university departments consented to accept the material for doctoral dissertations."[4]

Kinsey, like Freud, had to rely on secondhand data—the recollections and impressions of his subjects. According to his associates, Kinsey recognized, at the time of his death in 1956, the need for clinical observation of sexual intercourse. The same thought had occurred to Dr. William H. Masters, a physician and associate professor at the Washington University School of Medicine in St. Louis. In 1956, Masters and Mrs. Virginia E. Johnson, a psychologist, began to interview volunters for a laboratory study of the ways in which the human body responds to sexual stimulation.[5]

---

[2] Until recently, "all the best parts" of Krafft-Ebing were printed in Latin.

[3] Alfred C. Kinsey, Clyde E. Martin, Wardell B. Pomeroy, *Sexual Behavior in the Human Male* (1948).

[4] Edward Sagarin, "Taking Stock of Studies of Sex," *The Annals* (of the American Academy of Political and Social Science), March 1968, p. 2.

[5] Masters at first recruited prostitutes for research, believing them to be the only available subjects because of the taboo against public sexual performance. However, he found them unsuitable for an investigation of normal sexuality.

Sexual Revolution: Myth or Reality

Over a period of 11 years, 382 women and 312 men of ages 18 to 89 participated in the laboratory research stage of the Masters-Johnson project. The volunteers masturbated or copulated while their respiration, blood pressure, heartbeat, and other physiological responses were monitored and the visually significant aspects recorded on color film. Through such measurement and observation Masters and Johnson documented the reality and intensity of the female orgasm, demonstrated that there is no physiological difference between a clitoral and a vaginal orgasm, proved that many post-menopausal women have a strong sexual drive and that a man in his late seventies can be sexually effective.

Perhaps the most startling assertion of Masters and Johnson was that masturbation produces a more intense sexual response than does copulation. As they later put it: "The maximum physiologic intensity of orgasmic response subjectively reported or objectively recorded has been achieved by self-regulated mechanical or automanipulative technique. The next highest level of erotic intensity has resulted from partner manipulation, again with established or self-regulated methods, and the lowest intensity of target-organ response was achieved during coition."

Masters and Johnson managed to conduct their work in relative secrecy until the magazine *Commentary* published an article in November 1964 describing their project. Written by Dr. Leslie H. Farber, a psychiatrist in Washington, D. C., the article attacked Masters and Johnson as having dehumanized sex and disregarded its psychological aspects. Masters and Johnson reacted by suspending research and writing a book, *Human Sexual Response,* a year before they had intended to do so. Despite the ridicule of certain critics and some objections on moral grounds, *Human Sexual Response* generally was well received in the popular press and in medical journals. Their second major book, *Human Sexual Inadequacy,* was scheduled for publication in late April 1970.

Just as Kinsey paved the way for Masters and Johnson, the latter two apparently have opened the door to highly specialized sexual research. A recent example is *Tearoom Trade: Impersonal Sex in Public Places,* a study of sexual encounters between male homosexuals in public restrooms.[6]

---

[6] "Tearoom" is homosexual argot for a public restroom where sexual contacts are readily available.

The author, Laud Humphreys, an assistant professor of sociology at Southern Illinois University, gathered his data by posing as a "watchqueen"—a third man whose function is to warn of the approach of police or of a stranger. Humphreys recounted that he observed "hundreds of acts of fellatio" and recorded "15 of these encounters (involving 53 sexual acts) in great detail." [7] And an associate professor of sociology at City College of New York, Edward Sagarin, has related that one of his colleagues was "preparing to do a participant-observation study of 'wife-swapping.'"

Effect of Birth Control Pill on Sexual Behavior

Science and technology have helped to alter sexual attitudes and behavior by making available an inexpensive, almost totally effective contraceptive pill for women. However, some observers argue that The Pill was developed in response to changing sex attitudes instead of the other way around. Edward Grossman has said: "The grants to set up the labs would not have been awarded, the talent to synthesize the chemistry would not have been collected, if there had not been an agreement too deep . . . to be put into words . . ."

> It would be a state, and a state of mind, in which sex would be separated—as far as science, will and conscience could separate it— from duty, pain and fear, from everything but pleasure, and there would be an equality of giving pleasure and taking it, as in a mythic democracy where power would not be exercised by one group or person over another [i.e., by men over women]. [8]

In addition to facilitating family planning, The Pill has undermined the double standard of sexual morality. Liberated from the fear of unwanted pregnancy, women now possess the same freedom as men, in theory at least, to engage in premarital intercourse. It is difficult to determine how many women have taken advantage of this freedom, or how extensively. But various surveys indicate that premarital sexual activity has increased only slightly to moderately since The Pill went on the market in 1960. The increase may be greater among college students than among other groups of young people, although estimates and survey data vary widely. [9] Two New York University sociologists believe that

---

[7] Laud Humphreys, "Tearoom Trade: Impersonal Sex in Public Places," *Trans-Action*, January 1970, p. 15.

[8] Edward Grossman, "In Pursuit of the American Woman," *Harper's*, February 1970, p. 67. See "Oral Contraceptives," *E.R.R.*, 1966 Vol. II, p. 825.

[9] Arno Karlen reported in the *New York Times Magazine*, Jan. 26, 1969, that "40 years ago, 15-20 per cent of college girls were non-virgins; today the figure is about 25 per cent." Vance Packard asserted in *The Sexual Wilderness* (1968) that 43 per cent of college women were no longer virgins by age 21.

Sexual Revolution: Myth or Reality

"what The Pill does is to give sexual freedom to those who are having steady sexual relationships, for then the use of The Pill adds to romantic love by making elaborate preparations unnecessary." [10]

Steady sexual relationships without sanction of marriage appear to be more numerous—or at least more conspicuous—on certain college campuses today than formerly. Some of these "unmarried marrieds" eventually become man and wife, but many do not. The author of a study of these campus couples reports that, far from giving an impression of rebelliousness, they are "familiar, predictable and slightly boring." Among such young people, moreover, "there seems to be a trend toward passive males and controlling girls."

The male seems to be absolving himself of as much responsibility as he possibly can and the female, believing she makes herself more attractive, assumes more responsibility for herself and encourages him in his avoidance. It's related to a change in the family, and the devaluation of marriage. Being a man is a hell of a chore today, and many young men grow up very protected and a bit emasculated, with a somewhat feminine orientation. Being a wife is no more attractive to many of the girls than a 9-to-5 job is for the boys.[11]

Numerous colleges and universities distribute birth-control devices to both married and unmarried coeds who request them. Among the institutions that do so are the University of Michigan, the University of Chicago, the University of Illinois, Cornell, Yale—which admitted female undergraduates for the first time in 1969—Northwestern and the University of California campuses at Berkeley, Davis, Los Angeles, Santa Barbara and San Diego.

The safety of The Pill has recently been called into question by some physicians. Dr. Hugh J. Davis, a Johns Hopkins University gynecologist specializing in birth control devices, told a Senate subcommittee on Jan. 14, 1970, that the synthetic hormones contained in The Pill may cause breast cancer. British medical authorities had earlier concluded that women taking pills containing large amounts of synthetic estrogen ran the risk of serious, sometimes fatal, blood clotting. Davis recommended that healthy young women use The Pill for no more than two years. And he criticized the casual manner in which oral contraceptives sometimes are dis-

---

[10] Erwin O. Smigel and Rita Seiden, "The Decline and Fall of the Double Standard," *The Annals*, March 1968, p. 17.

[11] Arno Karlen, "The Unmarried Marrieds on Campus," *New York Times Magazine*, Jan. 26, 1969, pp. 29, 79.

pensed: "In many clinics The Pill has been served up as if it was chewing gum." [12] Such warnings apparently have been taken to heart. A poll taken by the Gallup Organization and printed in *Newsweek*, Feb. 9, 1970, indicated that 18 per cent of the approximately 8.5 million American women on The Pill had stopped using it. Moreover, 23 per cent were considering such action.

Reevaluation of Women's Sexual and Social Role

The sexual revolution is in essence a women's revolution. Old assumptions about the nature of female sexuality and women's place in society are being challenged—primarily by women themselves. Naomi Weisstein, an assistant professor of psychology at Loyola University (Chicago), has summed up the traditional American view of women as follows: "Our culture and our psychology characterize women as inconsistent, emotionally unstable, lacking in a strong superego, weaker, nurturant rather than productive, intuitive rather than intelligent, and—if they are at all normal—suited to the home and family. In short, the list adds up to a typical minority group stereotype—woman as nigger—if she knows her place (the home), she is really a quite lovable, loving creature, happy and childlike." [13]

The question is whether passiveness, both sexual and social, is congenital to women or if it has been forced upon them. Militant women's rights organizations such as the Radical Feminists, Women's International Terrorist Conspiracy from Hell (WITCH) and the Older [over 30] Women's Liberation naturally support the latter interpretation. It is argued that subordination of women arose historically from the need for a high birth rate to offset a high infant death rate. "To ensure a large family, a woman had to spend a good many years of her life in a state of pregnancy. Breeding was her major function. She was assured of status simply by having children, and little more was demanded of her." [14]

Today, of course, medical science has drastically reduced the infant mortality rate, at least in advanced countries. And while the birth rate has declined also, it remains sufficiently high to justify concern about a "population explosion." The

---

[12] Testimony before Senate Small Business Committee's Subcommittee on Monopoly.

[13] Naomi Weisstein, "Woman as Nigger," *Psychology Today*, October 1969, p. 58.

[14] Jessie Bernard, "Technology, Science and Sex Attitudes," *Impact*, October-December 1968, p. 215.

Pill gave women a way of avoiding pregnancy at a time when worry about overpopulation provided them with a socially valid reason for avoiding it. The Civil Rights Act of 1964 gave impetus to the women's equality movement by outlawing, almost as an afterthought, discrimination on the basis of sex in the field of employment.[15] Radical women's groups have been pressing for enforcement of this provision. For example, the Columbia Women's Liberation issued a report in January 1970 charging that the university employed female Ph.D.'s as part-time lecturers, whereas male Ph.D.'s who taught part-time were given professorial status.

In addition to demanding equal employment opportunities, the women's liberation movement is attempting to challenge the unspoken social demand that all women marry. A small but apparently growing number of women have elected to become "bachelor mothers"—that is, they have forsworn marriage even after giving birth to a child. Two prominent persons who have done so are actresses Mia Farrow and Vanessa Redgrave.

Agitation for full equality for women seems to have had an unsettling effect on many men. Rollo May has reported that an increasing number of male patients undergoing psychoanalysis complain of impotence. "Men feel like drone bees," he explains. "They mount the Queen Bee, or the liberated woman, from time to time, and wait to be eaten up." [16] It has been suggested also that some men are disturbed by indications that women's sexuality, once thought feeble, probably is stronger and more complex than that of men. "It would be galling," Edward Grossman wrote, "to have statistical proof that men possess a tiny fraction of the endowment of women to experience pleasure, and as if that were not enough, that women gain in potential as they age, while men lose."

Assertiveness of Male and Female Homosexuals

The militance of women's liberation groups is matched by that of a number of homosexual organizations, including the Gay Liberation Front, the Student Homophile League and the Pink Panthers. Homosexuals traditionally have devoted a great deal of effort to keeping their sexual inclinations a secret lest they lose their jobs or become vulnerable to black-

---

[15] See 1964 *Congressional Quarterly Almanac*, pp. 340-341.
[16] Quoted by Gail Sheehy, "A City Kind of Love," *New York*, Feb. 16, 1970, p. 30.

mail. But many younger homosexuals make no secret of the fact that they prefer members of their own sex, and they openly press their demands that legal and social strictures against homosexuality be eliminated.

The stereotype homosexual depicted on stage or screen is a pathetic figure—"a curio-shop proprietor with an uncertain mouth, wet basset eyes, a Coppertone tan and a miniature Yorkshire, who lives in a white and silver Jean Harlow apartment, drinks pink gin, cooks *boeuf Bourguignon,* mourns Judy [Garland], makes timid liaisons on Forty-second Street, gets mugged by midnight cowboys. . . ." The description no doubt fits numerous middle-aged homosexuals. But "the new homosexual of the seventies," it is said, is "an unfettered, guiltless male child of the new morality in a Zapata moustache and an outlaw hat, who couldn't care less for Establishment approval, would as soon sleep with boys as girls, and thinks that 'Over the Rainbow' is a place to fly on 200 grams of lysergic acid diethylamide [LSD]." [17]

Established homosexual organizations such as the Mattachine Society have worked quietly behind the scenes for years to overturn government regulations that bar employment of known homosexuals. [18] Newer groups take a more open approach. A student homosexual organization called Fight Repression of Erotic Expression (FREE) requested, and was accorded, recognition by the University of Minnesota in 1969. FREE then proceeded to hold the first of a series of dances in the student union. In the same year, the outraged patrons of a male gay bar in Greenwich Village pelted raiding New York City policemen with cans, bottles and coins. A series of nightly demonstrations followed, capped by a street march in which the participants carried a lavender banner proclaiming "Gay Power," chanted "Gay Power to Gay People" and sang "We Shall Overcome."

Organized activity appears to be increasing also among female homosexuals, who generally attract less attention and less opprobrium than their male counterparts. Attendance at meetings of the New York chapter of the Daughters of Bilitis, a nation-wide Lesbian organization, has tripled in

---

[17] Tom Burke, "The New Homosexuality," *Esquire,* December 1969, p. 178.

[18] See "Homosexuality: Morals and Security," *E.R.R.,* 1963 Vol. II, pp. 510-518. The federal government continues to refuse to hire known homosexuals on security grounds. The New York City Civil Service Commission announced last May, as a result of legal action brought against it by two men, that homosexuality was no longer a barrier to all jobs under its jurisdiction.

the past several years. A woman is chairman of the New York University Student Homophile League, and there are woman executive members of similar organizations at Cornell and Columbia.

Nevertheless, "straight" society continues to regard homosexuality with anxiety and contempt, as reflected in the numerous laws penalizing such activity. Illinois in 1961 became the first state to remove the penalty for homosexual relations in private between consenting adults. A similar law was approved in Connecticut in 1969 and will take effect in 1971. A panel of experts appointed by the National Institute of Mental Health recommended repeal of all statutes outlawing homosexual activity between consenting adults. The panel asserted, Oct. 20, 1969: "The extreme opprobrium that our society has attached to homosexual behavior, by way of criminal statutes and restrictive employment practices, has done more harm than good and goes beyond what is necessary for the maintenance of public order and human decency."

Nudity on Stage and Screen; Printed Pornography

Nowhere is the contemporary trend toward sexual permissiveness more evident than in the arts and entertainment field. The play *Marat/Sade* caused a minor sensation in the 1965-66 Broadway season when the audience was offered a brief glimpse of an actor's unclad backside. In the same season, Mayor John V. Lindsay had to intervene to prevent the city Department of Licenses from forcing female dancers of the Ballets Africains to perform in brassieres. Only four theater seasons later, almost all barriers against nudity and sexual expression in the New York theater had been leveled. Broadway and Off-Broadway plays featuring frontal male and female nudity and, in some cases, simulated sexual acts, have included *Oh! Calcutta!*, *Hair*, *Geese*, *And Puppy Dog Tails*, *Che!*,[19] and *Grin and Bare It!* The proliferation of such offerings led critic Eric Bentley to conclude that the main reason for theater-going in the late 1960s was "to see the penis." "The penis has an enormous dual audience: first, women, who after centuries of restraint have broken down

---

[19] All four members of the original cast of *Che!*, as well as the producer, the playwright and the light man, were convicted of obscenity in Manhattan Criminal Court on Feb. 25, 1970, for presenting what a three-judge panel called "a nadir of smut on the stage." In the play, actors had simulated intercourse, masturbation and defecation.

and confessed that this is what they wish to see; and secondly, homosexuals, or rather men with a marked homosexual component, which is more men than one used to think." [20]

Motion pictures have kept pace with the stage in the area of sexual explicitness. *I Am Curious (Yellow)*, a Swedish film that includes several scenes of intercourse, remains the best known of the sexually forthright movies even a year after its initial American release. But numerous other films, both foreign and American-made, are equally direct in their treatment of sex. Some examples are *Inga, Zabriskie Point, Coming Apart, Vixen*, and almost anything directed by Andy Warhol. Homosexuality once was a taboo subject on the screen, but no longer. *The Killing of Sister George* contained a scene depicting a sexual act between two women; *Midnight Cowboy*, based on a novel about a male prostitute, has been one of the most popular films released in the past year. The stage play *The Boys in the Band*, which depicts a birthday party attended by a group of male homosexuals, has been made into a motion picture.

The current crop of sexually explicit films has been made possible by a series of Supreme Court rulings that held prior censorship of motion pictures unconstitutional and severely limited the powers of state and local censors. Freed from such outside restraints, the American motion picture industry has instituted a rating program which, in effect, delegates to parents the decision of whether their children should see a given movie. Even the National Catholic Office for Motion Pictures, successor to the old Legion of Decency, has relaxed its once-stern standards. Thirty years ago, the Legion of Decency fought to keep Rhett Butler's punch line —"Frankly, Scarlett, I don't give a damn"—out of *Gone With the Wind;* when producer David O. Selznick refused to delete the line, the Legion gave the picture a rating of "B" ("morally objectionable in part for all"). Richard Corliss noted that in 1969, however, *Beyond the Law*, a Norman Mailer melodrama with four-letter words galore, was granted the "B" rating while the reissue of *Gone With the Wind* was reclassified A-II, "unobjectionable for adults and adolescents." [21]

[20] Eric Bentley, "The Naked American," *The New Republic*, Aug. 9 & 16, 1969, p. 32.
[21] Richard Corliss, "Still Legion, Still Decent?" *Commonweal*, May 23, 1969, p. 288. See "Movies as Art," *E.R.R.*, 1969 Vol. I, pp. 416-417.

Printed pornography has developed into a major industry in the same period in which stage and screen sexual taboos have all but disappeared. The fragmented and shadowy nature of the erotica trade makes its size difficult to estimate; but sales are believed to total between $500 million and $2 billion a year. *The New York Times* reported Feb. 22, 1970, in a survey of pornography as "big business" that theaters across the country showing "sexploitation" movies numbered about 600, a tenfold increase in five years. "Adult" book stores have proliferated from New York to Los Angeles, the twin centers of pornography production in the United States. Every sexual taste is catered to with books, movies, magazines, records, photographs and artificial sex organs. The Post Office Department reported that in 1969 it received 232,000 complaints from persons who received unsolicited pornographic literature, more than twice as many complaints as received two years earlier. President Nixon, in a special message sent to Congress on May 2, 1969, proposed legislation aimed at curbing the flow of materials sent through the mails. More than 200 anti-obscenity bills have been introduced in Congress. But not everyone agrees with Nixon's contention that pornography constitutes a "social evil," and the Supreme Court has had trouble defining it.[22]

Changes in Sexual Mores Through History

A REVOLUTION is by definition an overthrow of the existing order of things. In the case of the current sexual revolution—if indeed it is a revolution—the tottering structure of Victorianism is the target. Victorianism, in turn, was a reaction against the licentiousness of the 18th century. Throughout history, sexual mores have fluctuated between the extremes of permissiveness and repression—not only from time to time but also from society to society. The author of a study of American sex attitudes has noted that no type of sexual activity has not been held permissible at some time in human history, including rape, bestiality and incest. "Equally, there is no type of sexual behavior which has not been taboo at one time or another, with the possible

---

[22] See "First Amendment and the Mass Media," *E.R.R.*, 1970 Vol. I, pp. 54-55, and "Changes in Moral Customs and Laws," *E.R.R.*, 1965 Vol. II, pp. 499-522.

exception of genital contact between husband and wife."
"What is unusual about Western Christendom," he added,
"is that it has proscribed so many sexual activities, and
sometimes has attempted to proscribe *all sexual activity*." [23]

The groundwork of Victorianism was laid in medieval
times by the Christian church. Church doctrine called for
celibacy when possible, to the point where wives were encouraged to deny their husbands. Outside of marriage, sex
was everywhere forbidden. Church pronouncements on sex
appear to have been honored more in the breach than in the
observance in the Middle Ages. The chivalry of knights in
King Arthur's time was largely fictitious, according to Rat-
tray Taylor in *Sex in History*. "The fact of the matter was
that knights routinely raped any woman they found in the
woods." In the 14th century, he added, "women wore low-
necked dresses, so tight around the hips as to reveal their
sex, and laced their breasts so high that, as was said, 'a
candle could be stood upon them.'" Furthermore, "Men
wore short coats, revealing their private parts, which were
clearly outlined by a glove-like container known as a
braguette."

It is commonly supposed that sexual activity was severely
restricted in the early Puritan settlements of New England.
Church and court records of the time indicate that this impression is only partly accurate. Puritan leaders openly
praised sexual relations within marriage and decried the
"Popish conceit of the excellence of virginity." Gov. William
Bradford complained in 1642 of the incontinence of both
married and unmarried persons in Plymouth Colony; records of 17th century New England courts show that forni-
cation and adultery constituted by far the most numerous
class of criminal cases that came to trial.

Pervasiveness of Sexual Prudery in 19th Century

In 18th century America, Arthur C. Calhoun wrote in *A
Social History of the American Family* (1917), sexual
morality was "a very scarce commodity among people of the
ruling class." Alexander Hamilton was able to remain in
office despite involvement in an adultery scandal. Benjamin
Franklin raised his bastard son in his own household, and
he took his bastard grandchild to Europe as his secretary.

---

[23] James L. Collier, *The Hypocritical American* (1964), pp. 6-7.

Sexual Revolution: Myth or Reality

The 19th century saw the rise of Victorianism, an all-inclusive system of morality named for the queen who succeeded to the English throne in 1837. Victorian morality was stern and family-oriented, with overtones of prudery and of respectability for respectability's sake. Nineteenth-century Englishmen believed that "To abstain from gambling, to remember the Sabbath day, to keep it holy, to limit the gratification of the senses to the pleasures of a table lawfully earned and the embraces of a wife lawfully wedded, are virtues for which the reward is not laid up in heaven only." They waged unremitting war on impropriety, for "an unguarded look, a word, a gesture, a picture, a novel, might plant a seed of corruption in the most innocent heart." [24] Puritan sexual strictures applied only to pre- and extramarital activity. The Victorians went considerably further, James L. Collier wrote, in that they "did not even consider [sex] good in the marriage bed."

It was unfortunately necessary; it was just too bad that men were basically lustful beasts. Sex was not to be talked about, even in the most peripheral way. Legs became limbs, and piano legs were sometimes dressed in pantaloons to conceal them. Women, moreover, were not supposed to enjoy sex, in fact were assumed not even to know it existed. Men were supposed to contain their impulses as well as they could. Our whole intense system of schoolboy athletics, around which our cult of sports was built, was developed by the Victorians specifically to work off sexual energy in hopes of keeping young men from masturbating. At least partly for the same reason sea bathing in cold water became popular, and the cult of ocean and beach was created.

Victorian morality had a profound influence on sexual attitudes in both the United States and England. Its effect on sexual behavior probably was considerably less, although no definitive study of the subject has been made. It is known, however, that cities such as London, New York, San Francisco and New Orleans supported extraordinarily large numbers of prostitutes in the late 19th century. One contemporary estimate placed the number of prostitutes in New York in 1880 at 60,000—roughly one for every 15 adult males in the city.

Freud's Influence and Retreat from Victorianism

Victorian sexual morality held sway until the 1920s, when it began to crumble under the impact of social changes wrought by World War I. "The soldier who went abroad had

---

[24] G. M. Young, *Victorian England: Portrait of an Age* (1953), p. 13.

new sexual experiences and came in contact with women whose behavior derived from different and more permissive sex norms; the returned veteran brought back with him sexual attitudes shaped by these new norms." [25] Young women went to work in factories and thereby gained a taste of economic independence. At the same time the women's suffrage movement was in full swing, and Margaret Sanger had begun her pioneering work in dispensing birth-control information. Mass production of the automobile and increasing urbanization afforded young people of the 1920s more privacy than their parents had enjoyed.

Data gathered by Lewis M. Ternan in a 1938 study of *Psychological Factors in Marital Happiness* pointed to a significant change in American sexual behavior around the time of World War I. Ternan found that only 26 per cent of females born between 1890 and 1899 had engaged in premarital intercourse, as compared with 49.8 per cent of those born between 1900 and 1909.[26] His figures showed a similar though less dramatic trend among men: 58.1 per cent of male interviewees born between 1890 and 1899 said they had had premarital coitus, as compared with 67.4 per cent of those born between 1900 and 1909. "Clearly, the major change in sex practices occurred in the generation . . . which came of sexual age during or immediately after World War I, a period characterized by marked social change and innovation."

Freud's writings about the unconscious and the effect of sex on personality are believed to have contributed greatly to the revolution of sexual mores in the 1920s. Among other things, Freud affirmed the existence of female sexuality, which the Victorians had denied, and he demonstrated that suppression of sexual desires could lead to mental disturbances. As a result, Rollo May wrote, "The belief became a militant dogma in liberal circles that the opposite of repression—namely, sex education, freedom of talking, feeling, and expression—would have healthy effects, and obviously constituted the only stand for the enlightened person." Today, May added, "far from not talking about sex, we might well seem, to a visitor from Mars dropping into Times Square, to have no other topic of communication."

[25] Erwin O. Smigel and Rita Seiden, *op. cit.*, p. 10.
[26] Alfred C. Kinsey independently reported almost identical figures in *Sexual Behavior in the Human Female* (1953).

Persistence of Anxiety About Sexuality

ADVOCATES of greater sexual freedom have usually argued that it would lead to greater personal happiness. But evidence abounds that anxiety about sex still persists, though perhaps for different reasons than formerly. Large numbers of people continue to consult psychiatrists about sexual problems, sex crimes are steadily increasing, and sex education courses in many localities have come under bitter attack. Ira L. Weiss, an Iowa sociologist, goes so far as to assert that the sexual revolution is a myth and the only basic change is a trend toward more equality between the sexes. "There has been less change than [is] popularly believed between modern American males and their Victorian grandfathers." [27]

Leopold Tyrmand, a Polish essayist now living in the United States, believes that the atmosphere of "anything-goes" is destructive of sexuality. "No longer than a decade ago," Tyrmand has written, "bemused Americans discovered that sex is simply a part of the eternal human condition, like everything else, grief and anguish included—that it may encompass casualness and tragedy, mischievous grotesquerie and distasteful tawdriness, random little dramas and lifelong goals, permanent enigmas, endless agonies, convoluted mysteries, and nondescript perfection. Engulfing this newly acquired sensitivity in a chaotic tide of permissiveness might prove to be the American crime of the century." [28]

Numerous authorities have stated that marriage manuals and other books designed to improve sexual technique have made sex so mechanized, detached and intellectual that it was robbed of its sensuality. "Man became a spectator of his own sexual experience," Susan Lydon wrote. "And the marriage manuals put new pressure on women. The swing was from repression to preoccupation with orgasm." [29] Rollo May has expressed similar views. In his opinion, "There is an inverse relationship between the number of how-to-do-it books perused by a person or rolling off the presses in a

---

[27] Quoted in *New York Times*, Oct. 22, 1967.
[28] Leopold Tyrmand, "Reflections—Permissiveness and Rectitude," *The New Yorker*, Feb. 28, 1970, p. 88.
[29] Susan Lydon, "Understanding Orgasm," *Ramparts*, Dec. 14-28, 1968, p. 62.

society and the amount of sexual passion or even pleasure experienced by the persons involved."

"Whatever merits or failings the Kinsey studies and the Masters-Johnson research have in their own right," May added, "they are symptomatic of a culture in which the personal meaning of love has been progressively lost." Love and passion appear to have become more elusive as sex has become more available. The observation of a Frenchman, Raoul de Roussy de Sales, in 1938 is still pertinent: "America appears to be the only country in the world where love is a national problem." *Playboy* magazine has achieved success with its female nude center-spreads, its bawdy cartoons, jokes and stories, and its "Playboy Philosophy" celebrating the advantages of sexual liberation. Still, the magazine has been attacked on the same ground that sex manuals have been attacked—for being basically anti-sexual. "The irony is that large numbers of those who purchase the *Playboy* product secretly believe that sex really is bad. . . . The vicarious sexual involvement and stimulation which some find in the world of unreality between the covers of such magazines bears testimony to their continued bondage to 'sex is bad' thinking and to the absence of genuine sexual involvement in their lives." [30]

The author of a recent book has suggested that the scarcity of time in modern society has made the lengthy love affair all but obsolete. "Modern love affairs are reminiscent . . . of business agreements: 'No frills, [no] flowers, no time wasted in elaborate compliments, verses, and lengthy seductions, no complications, and no scenes, please.' " [31]

Sex Education Controversy in the Public Schools

The current uproar over sex education in public schools lends support to the argument that the sexual revolution is not so widespread as it might seem. Most sex education classes in the schools have been introduced since 1964, the year that the Sex Information and Education Council of the U. S. (SIECUS) was established as "a clearinghouse of information on sex." The council set itself the goal of dignifying sex "by openness of approach, study and scientific research designed to lead toward its understanding and its freedom from exploitation."

---

[30] Frederic C. Wood Jr., *Sex and the New Immorality* (1968), pp. 35-36.
[31] Staffan Burenstam Linder, *The Harried Leisure Class* (1970), p. 85.

From the beginning, SIECUS promoted sex education in the public schools. It argued that instruction should start before students are old enough to become emotionally involved in the subject and that the curriculum should attempt to describe not only the human reproductive process but also the effect of sex on personality, family, and society. Sex education spread to around 50 per cent of the country's schools—both public and private, parochial and nonsectarian—by the end of 1968.

Then an unexpected storm of protest broke. Its source is believed to be a pamphlet by a writer named Gordon Drake, a former member of the John Birch Society who had joined the Christian Crusade. Entitled *Is the School House the Proper Place to Teach Raw Sex?*, the pamphlet implied that sex education was (1) harmful, in that it could lead to immoral behavior; (2) un-American, in that it invaded the sanctity of the home; (3) un-Christian, in that it provided no moral guidance. The pamphlet is reported to have sold around 50,000 copies almost immediately after publication.

Sex education was opposed on different grounds also. Some parents regarded it as a threat to the child's so-called latency period (ages 6 through 12 years) during which, according to Freud, he submerges sexual interests and concentrates on play and learning. Others questioned whether schools were capable of instructing a child in so delicate a subject as sex. If schools couldn't teach Johnny to read, it was argued, could they be trusted to tell him about sex? Organized opposition to sex education in schools had appeared in at least 27 states by early 1970. As yet there is no consensus on the meaning and purpose of sex education.[32] The controversy over sex education is likely to continue for some time. The real test may come when a new generation of parents, supposedly infused with ideas of sexual permissiveness, have children of their own attending schools that offer sex instruction.

The sexual revolution now being fought in the United States was fought and won long ago in Denmark and Sweden. In both countries premarital sex relations are openly accepted; pornography may be freely printed and sold; and virtually all laws against such sexual aberrations as homo-

---

[32] John Kobler, "Sex Invades the Schoolhouse," *The Saturday Evening Post*, June 29, 1968, p. 66.

sexuality, transvestism and group sex have been abolished. The Scandinavian experience may therefore be instructive for Americans. The lifting of restrictions on pornography apparently has done little in Denmark or Sweden except to foster a booming export industry.[33] Denmark, which dropped all legal barriers against printed pornography in July 1967 and all barriers against photographic pornography in July 1969, has reported a sharp decrease in sex crimes. Police authorities disclosed on Jan. 2, 1970, that 31 per cent fewer sexual offenses were reported in 1969 than in 1968 in metropolitan Copenhagen and 50 per cent fewer in Aarhus, the country's second largest city. Police and criminologists pointed out, however, that fewer arrests for public indecency, voyeurism, male prostitution and, significantly, sale of pornographic material, accounted almost exclusively for the decrease. Danish authorities hesitate to credit legalization of pornography with the decline in sex crimes.

Pictorial pornography likewise is taken in stride in Sweden. "I doubt that pornography is turning any Swedes on to sex," American literary critic Susan Sontag commented. "Its prevalence seems rather one more barrier to eroticism, one more hurdle the Swede has to jump before he can be fully inside his own feelings, his own skin."[34] Sex education has been mandatory in Swedish schools since 1956, and is now being made mandatory in Danish schools. Sexual morality apparently has not suffered as a result. Denmark's rate of out-of-wedlock births, 11.2 per cent in 1968, is about the same as it was 150 years ago, to judge from church records of the period. And the venereal disease rate of 2.2 per 1,000 Danish youths between the ages of 16 and 19 is believed to be only one-tenth as great as in New York City.

The Scandinavian experience, in short, would seem to indicate that public permissiveness has comparatively little effect on private sexual behavior. It is far from certain, however, that Americans would react like Danes or Swedes to the removal of sexual taboos. The sexual revolution in Scandinavia began decades ago, when Victorian morality still held sway in the United States. Progress toward sexual liberation in this country thus promises to be slow and painful, and accompanied by controversy every step of the way.

---

[33] West Germany, Britain, and the United States are reported to be the world's leading purchasers of pornography on a per capita basis.

[34] Susan Sontag, "A Letter From Sweden," *Ramparts*, July 1969, p. 31.

THE OCCULT VS. THE CHURCHES

by

Ralph C. Deans

1 9 7 0
Apr. 24

THE OCCULT VS. THE CHURCHES

DESPITE THE RATIONALISM of society today, and perhaps partly because of it, belief in occult matters not only persists but is growing. Many theologians and social thinkers are worried about the new interest Americans show in astrology, mediums and seances, witches covens, Satanism and black masses. There is abundant evidence that millions of persons half-believe, are willing to believe or do indeed believe in mysterious forces that are dismissed by science and most Western religions as superstition.

The present "occult boom" seems to have tapped a hidden reservoir of the mind. Classes in the history of witchcraft, sorcery and the black arts are being taught in many high schools and universities, and they are usually over-enrolled. Bookstore shelves are laden with occult books, both sensational and academic. More than 1,200 daily newspapers in the United States publish columns on astrology for upward of 40 million readers, whose interest may range from that of casual diversion to wholehearted commitment.

Toy manufacturers report that the closest thing to a trend in playthings being readied for sale next Christmas involve astrology, witchcraft, and other aspects of the supernatural. *Rosemary's Baby,* a best-selling novel by Ira Levin about witchcraft, was made into a movie that had grossed $15 million by the end of 1969 and placed 38th on *Variety's* list of all-time "boxoffice champs." Jeane Dixon, who claims a gift of prophecy, has sold more than three million copies of her books.

"The Age of Aquarius is not only a song in a rock musical (*Hair*), but a cause of economic celebration in our department stores and spiritual fulfillment on our campuses."[1] The revival of occultism has also had a darker side. Charles Manson, who has been charged in connection with the murders of actress

---

[1] Nicholas Pileggi, "Occult," *McCall's,* March 1970, p. 63. The magazine devoted almost its entire issue to a discussion of occult matters.

Sharon Tate and six others in Los Angeles in August 1969, "seemed to consider himself something of a prophet and even a savior."[2] His worshipful "family" of hippies, most of them young women, believed he had mysterious powers and obeyed him without question. Sirhan B. Sirhan was reported to have been deeply involved in Rosicrucianism[3] before he assassinated Robert F. Kennedy in June 1968.

Yearnings for Mysticism Outside Religion

In a recent interview with theologian Harvey Cox, editor T George Harris of *Psychology Today* magazine began by commenting on "the general resurgence of superstition and magic." Explanations for the resurgence are many and varied. Cox, an author and professor at Harvard Divinity School, offers a view that festivity and mystical celebration have disappeared from religion and that people are searching elsewhere for those experiences.[4]

Ludwig B. Lefebre, a psychotherapist, wrote in the same magazine in November 1968 that churches fail to respond to people seeking "to get beyond themselves." "Some churches," he said, "are aware of the current challenge but are not responding adequately." Persons attracted to LSD and other mind-expanding drugs seek what churches do not provide. The fundamental aim of those persons is spiritual, though misguided, "and their ultimate goal is direct contact of a revelatory nature with a suprahuman agency." The Rev. David H. C. Read, pastor of the Madison Avenue Presbyterian Church in New York, offers a similar assessment. "The revolt against the secular and materialistic society is in full swing amongst the young," he said, "and the traditional signs of yearning for the transcendent—apocalyptic imagery, ecstasy, symbolism, communes of withdrawal—are all around us."[5]

"The fascination of many Americans with Unidentified Flying Objects led some of them into the world of psychic phenomena," Nicholas Pileggi commented. "Certainly the whole metaphysical mixed bag of Eastern thought, so popular just a few years ago, helped create a climate for an interest in the occult. Yoga exercises, Zen mysteries, macrobiotic diets and

---

2 Steven V. Roberts, "Charlie Manson: One Man's Family," *New York Times Magazine*, Jan. 4, 1970, p. 32.

3 Rosicrucian societies date from the 17th century as mystical orders for possessing and passing on secret wisdom.

4 "Religion in The Age of Aquarius," *Psychology Today*, April 1970, p. 47.

5 Speech to the John Courtney Murray forum, New York, April 8, 1970.

spiritual fasts, even Karate launched many a middle-class mystic."[6] Rollo May, a veteran psychotherapist, has sought to explain the revival of superstition in terms of human experience in times of transition, like the present, "when the customary psychic defenses are weak or broken down entirely." May described these periods as "a time of actual fear among people of witchcraft, sorcerers, and others who claimed to know how to consort with demons."[7]

Attitude of Churches Toward the Occult Arts

As defined in its broadest sense by *Webster's New International Dictionary,* the occult encompasses anything "beyond the scope of plain understanding; mysterious, supernormal or supernatural." The term occult is applied to hundreds of practices, many of which purport to foretell future events. These range from the well-known, like astrology and palmistry, to the esoteric, like watching a rooster pick up grain (Alectryomancy); watching a water fountain in a mirror (Catoptromancy, also known as Pegomancy); and watching pearls thrown on a flat surface (Margaritomancy). There are such grisly forms as Hepatoscopy, that of studying the liver of a sacrificed sheep, and Hieromancy, that of studying the entrails of animals.

Most churches traditionally have opposed all such forms of divination. The Bible denounces occult practices but implicit in all biblical denunciations is the belief that magic works. The New Testament recounts numerous miracles, including the raising of the dead. The *Catholic Encyclopaedia* notes that the Roman Catholic Church "does not deny that, with a special permission of God, the souls of the departed may appear to the living, and even manifest things unknown..."

The Catholic Church holds that it is possible, under some circumstances, for the devil or evil spirits to literally "possess" a human being. The 1947 New York edition of the *Ritual Romanum* (rituals of the Roman Catholic Church), with an introduction by the late Francis Cardinal Spellman, reproduced the ancient rite of exorcism in Latin. Instruction 20 advised the exorcist to "ask the devil if he was forced into the body of the possessed person by some trick or magic or an evil spell, or potion, which if the possessed has taken by mouth he should be made to vomit up."[8]

---

6 Nicholas Pileggi, *op. cit.* p. 64. See "Eastern Religions and Western Man," *E.R.R.*, 1969 Vol. I, pp. 446-449.

7 Rollo May, *Love And Will* (1969), p. 129.

8 *Ritual Romanum* (1947), pp. 326-347. The translation comes from a foreword written by Felix Morrow (p. xii) in the *History of Witchcraft,* a book by Montague Summers.

Although the Catholic church believes it is possible for man to have direct experience with both good and evil spirits, it is extremely cautious about pronouncing itself on any manifestations of the supernatural. The appearance of the Virgin Mary to Bernadette Soubirous at Lourdes, France, in 1858 was not accepted by the church until 1862 when the local bishop sanctioned belief in the apparitions.

Conservative churchmen see the modern interest in the occult as "ungodly" and perhaps sinful. The more moderate are likely to believe that it is potentially damaging spiritually and psychologically. A few liberal or radical church officials see potential good as well as evil in it. A spokesman for the Catholic Information Center in Washington, D.C., told Editorial Research Reports: "Our advice to young people is to stay away from it, it's dangerous."

Bishop Pike and Spiritualism; Scientific Inquiry

The late James A. Pike, a former Episcopal Bishop of California, saw matters differently. He became convinced before his own death that he had received messages from his dead son through spiritualist mediums. Pike had previously resigned his bishopric, in 1966, after church officials accused him of heresy for criticizing basic doctrines. After his son James Jr. had committed suicide in New York the same year, he began to notice pins and other objects arranged in strange positions in his room. Pike interpreted this as a sign that his dead son was trying to communicate with him. He visited spiritualist mediums over a period of months and expressed belief that, through their help, he had indeed contacted his son.

Pike permitted a Toronto station to tape and televise a seance in which he participated. The telecast, in September 1967, became the most publicized spiritualist event of recent years. Answering criticism of this action, he said: "Having been under a cloud for believing too little, it is at least a change to be faulted for believing too much."[9] Sydney E. Ahlstrom, professor of church history and American history at Yale, contends that the movement of Bishop Pike "from Episcopal neo-orthodoxy through Christian radicalism to spiritualism" symbolized a prominent tendency of the times in man's

---

9 James A. Pike, with Diane Kennedy, *The Other Side: An Account of My Experiences With Psychic Phenomena* (1968). Pike, divorced by his second wife, married Miss Kennedy in 1968. She was with him on a spiritualist pilgrimage to Palestine the following year when their automobile became stranded in the desert and he died in an unsuccessful attempt to find help. She survived.

PARAPSYCHOLOGY TERMS AND MEANINGS

Parapsychology: The study of human experience that by its very nature defies explanation in physical terms.

Extrasensory perception: The ability to know something that does not seem to involve any physical senses or rational inference.

Telepathy: Extrasensory perception of thoughts and mental states in another person.

Clairvoyance: Extrasensory perception of objects and events, as distinguished from thoughts and mental states of persons.

PSI: A general term (pronounced "sigh") for those things which parapsychologists study.

Psychokinesis (PK): The direct mental influence on a physical object.

Precognition: Extrasensory perception of a future event.

Retrocognition: Extrasensory perception of a past event.

---

quest for "untraditional" forms of religion. [10]

Rationalists tend to believe that those persons who offer themselves as spiritualist mediums have a highly developed intuitive sense. They can pick up clues from the person who seeks to make contact with the dead and use powers of suggestion to satisfy him. Nevertheless, parapsychologists have intensively studied purportedly spiritualistic occurrences. The existence of telepathy, clairvoyance, precognition, and psychokinesis all have been established, on a statistical basis, to the satisfaction of most scientists. There is, however, no universally acceptable explanation of these powers. "The attempts to explain parapsychological phenomena in terms of physical causes are as unsatisfactory as the supernatural claims of the occultist," parapsychologist Koneru Ramakrishna Rao has written. [11]

Centers for the study of experiences (called psi phenomena) are functioning at the City University of New York, St. Joseph's College in Philadelphia, the University of Virginia and the J.B. Rhine Laboratory in North Carolina, formerly associated with Duke University, where much of the pioneering research took place in the United States. In addition, Maimonides Hospital in Brooklyn conducts a Dream Laboratory for investigation of clairvoyance and precognition in dreams.

---

[10] Sydney E. Ahlstrom, "The Radical Turn in Theology and Ethics: Why It Occurred in the 1960s," *Annals* (of the American Academy of Political and Social Science), January 1970, p. 13.

[11] Koneru Ramakrishna Rao, *Experimental Parapsychology* (1966), p. 172.

The Supernatural: Profane and Divine

BELIEF IN THE SUPERNATURAL is at the heart of all major religions, East and West. The existence of some form of life after death is a basic tenet of virtually every major faith. In Christian belief, the transformation of bread and wine into the body and blood of Christ in Holy Communion is a miraculous event. Christian dogma also holds it possible for human beings to have extraordinary spiritual experiences, such as the flash of illumination which occurred to Saint Paul on the road to Damascus.

Many anthropologists assert that belief in supernatural forces is so universal that it must be instinctive. In every age, including the present, man has sought the ability to control these forces through mystical means, whether divine or profane. Since ancient times the priests and prophets of religion have been quick to condemn others who proclaimed similar powers. Until modern times it was never argued that a competing body of doctrine invoking the supernatural did not work, but only that it was evil. Injunctions against rival practices are found throughout the Old Testament. As related in the King James Version of the book of Deuteronomy, Moses told the children of Israel:

> There shall not be found among you any one that maketh his son or daughter to pass through the fire, or that useth divination, or an observer of times, or an enchanter, or a witch.
>
> Or a charmer, or a consulter with familiar spirits, or a wizard, or a necromancer.
>
> For all that do these things are an abomination unto God.

Enchanters, witches, charmers and all the rest persisted nevertheless and their arts flourished, especially in Europe during the Middle Ages when paradoxically religious belief had never been stronger. "Religions are born and may die," Will and Ariel Durant wrote in their appraisal of world civilization, "but superstition is immortal." [12] Superstition further survived the 18th century enlightenment to bloom anew today in the most technically advanced nation on earth. Self-styled

---

12 Will and Ariel Durant, *The Age of Reason Begins* (Part VII of *The Story of Civilization* series), p. 575.

witches of the 20th century blur the distinction between superstition and religion. They may call piously on God for
protection or they may try to conjure up a batch of demons.

Antiquity of Magic; Its Purposes and Methods

High magicians, if books on the subject are to be believed,
subject themselves to years of study and severe mental disci-
plines to master their art. Their aim is said to be nothing less
than attainment of cosmic power over all forces in the world.
Magic, according to historian Richard Cavendish, "is a titanic
attempt to exalt the stature of man, to put man in the place
which religious thought reserves for God."[13] The true magician
is presumed to know astrology, numerology, alchemy, the
mystic doctrine of the Cabala, and the spells, incantations
and instructions found in a dozen ancient textbooks, or
Grimoires.[14] He has gone through a lengthy, demanding ap-
prenticeship at the feet of a master magician. With the aid of
magical clothing and equipment, armed by magic weapons of
his own making, protected by a magic circle, the magician can
raise up powerful spirits who will do his bidding. The magician
does not supplicate, the texts add, he commands.

The Cabala is a mystifying and obscure doctrine said by its
adherents to have been handed down secretly since the time
of Abraham, to whom it was revealed by God. While the important parts are said to be transmitted from generation to
generation secretly, there are published sections of the belief.
These include the *Sepher Yetzirah* (Book of Formation) in
Hebrew, which may have been written in the third century A.D.,
and the *Zohar,* in Aramaic, probably written about 1275. According to the Cabala, God is the total of all things, good and
evil. His relation to the material world is indirect, working
through 10 "emanations" of himself called *sephiroth.* It is the
magician's intent to travel from sephiroth to sephiroth in an
"astral body" which he learns to control through self-improve-
ment. The magicians fear countless numbers of spirits which
guard each sephiroth and which will try to prevent him from
finally attaining union with God.

Much magical doctrine is of impenetrable obscurity. Most
of it derives from antiquity; although there are modern texts

---

13 Richard Cavendish, *The Black Arts,* (1967), p. 1.

14 The most famous of these is the *Key of Solomon,* supposedly written by King Solomon. A version in the British Museum is believed to date from the 12th century. Many
of the other *Grimoires* are based on it. The *Testament of Solomon,* in Greek, another
text book on magic, dates from 100-400 A.D.

they [15] draw heavily on the old. Many refer to God, but usually as an exceptionally strong spirit. A basic tenet is that the magician must not shirk "evil." To be fully effective, the texts suggest, a magician must know evil, cruelty and pain as well as goodness, mercy and pleasure. In magical thought, everything is "linked" together; "As below, so above," is how it is commonly expressed. The "unreal" things manipulated by the magician are supposed to have an impact on "real" things.

Similar relationships are drawn between the seen and the unseen, good and evil, and visible and invisible. Another belief is that everything has a "force" or "vibration"—which must be controlled if the magician is to be effective. Still another belief is that the "real" name of a thing controls that thing. The magician must know a host of secret "names of power" in order to call up spirits and to protect himself from them. One of the most powerful is the *Tetragrammaton,* or personal name of God, usually translated as Jehovah in the Bible. *Tetragrammaton* and other names of God—including Yah, Elohim, Sabaoth—are frequently used in magical incantations. A magician fears that a mispronounced word in an incantation can, through the magical "law of return," cause the conjured spirit to attack him.

Many of these ideas operate in the use of effigies, a familiar magical device often associated with West Indian Voodoo practices. A wax image constructed in the proper way "becomes" the person it represents. Pins stuck into it cause him pain; burning it causes him fever; and burying it causes him illness until it is dug up. "The belief that one is a victim of witchcraft is psychologically as potent as actual magic could be," anthropologist Elizabeth E. Bacon wrote in the *Encyclopedia Americana* (1968).

Spells and Incantations; Numerology and Tarot

Incantations are usually long and complicated. This excerpt which Cavendish translated from one of the *Grimoires* is intended to raise several spirits:

> By the dreadful Day of Judgement, by the Sea of Glass which is before the face of the Divine Majesty, by the four beasts before the Throne, having eyes before and behind, by the Fire which is about the Throne, by the Holy Angels of heaven and the Mighty Wisdom

---

[15] Perhaps the most popular is Aleister Crowley's *Magick in Theory and Practice,* published in Paris in 1929. Others published in the late 19th century and early 20th century include *Transcendental Magic, Its Doctrine and Ritual* and *The Key of the Mysteries* by Eliphas Levi (whose real name was Alphonse Constant), and *The Book of the Sacred Magic of Abramelin the Mage* and other works by S. L. Mathers.

of God. By the seal of Basdathea, by the name Primematum which Moses uttered and the earth opened and swallowed up Corah, Dathan and Abiram, answer all my demands and perform all that I desire. Come peaceably, visibly and without delay!

In a classic conjuring, the magician draws a magic circle nine feet in diameter. A second circle eight feet in diameter is drawn within the first and "names of power" written on the rim. Crosses, bowls of water and other things repugnant to devils are also placed in the rim. A brazier is lit inside the inner circle to attract spirits and provide them with smoke to make visible forms.

Many conjurings call for sacrifices, usually an animal but sometimes a human being—at least in theory. Aleister Crowley, a self-professed magician who died in 1947, recommended the sacrifice of "a male child of perfect innocence and high intelligence" for the performance of very high magic. Crowley, who was known as "the most evil man in the world" in his time, was expelled from several countries for unsavory practices—though none included the sacrifice of human beings. Actual human sacrifice in conjuring has been exceedingly rare since ancient times, as well as can be determined.

There is also "low magic." At its simplest, low magic is merely a knowledge of herbs. In medieval times such knowledge was enough to convict a person of witchcraft. Many plants and herbs were believed to have magical properties. The most powerful was the poisonous *atropa mandragora* or mandrake, which was used frequently in love potions. Low magic may include spells, incantations and conjurings but it is distinct from "high magic" because the user subordinates himself to the supernatural forces and demons he deals with. According to directions found in one of the old *Grimoires,* beans are placed in a human skull. It is then buried and the burial site is drenched with brandy for seven days. On the eighth day, the spirit of the dead person arrives and asks to pour the brandy. On the ninth day, the beans are taken from the skull and placed in the mouth of the person who initiated this rite. If the rite has been performed correctly, he then becomes invisible.

Numerology, one of the main occult "sciences," probably derives from the findings of Pythagoras four centuries before the birth of Christ. Basically, modern numerologists assign a value to every letter of the alphabet. They do not agree about the value of each letter, however. In one system, the letters have these values:

1	2	3	4	5	6	7	8	9
A	B	C	D	E	F	G	H	I
J	K	L	M	N	O	P	Q	R
S	T	U	V	W	X	Y	Z	

To determine personal character, numbers derived from letters are added in three combinations. The letters forming the name Richard M. Nixon, for example, add up to 78. The seven and eight are then added; the sum (15) yields a one and a five. Together they add up to six, the final magical number in this instance. The six-character in this system is said to be balanced, well-adjusted and placid. Six-people are said to be efficient, hard-working and perhaps dull.

There are several references to numerology in the Bible. The most famous is probably the beast described in the book of *Revelation*: "Here is wisdom. Let him that hath understanding count the number of the beast: for it is the number of a man; and his number is Six hundred three-score and six (666)." Numerologists have been looking for the beast for some time, sometimes identifying it with any public figure or institution whose names somehow form the figures 666. Jehovah's Witnesses, who form a modern-day religious sect, maintain that the Beast may be the political organization of the world at any given time.

Another body of magical thought has been handed down from obscure antiquity in the form of tarot cards, from which modern playing cards are derived. A tarot (rhymes with carrot) deck has 14 cards in each of four suits called swords, cups, pentacles and wands. In addition, there are 21 trump cards, each depicting a different scene; a fool, death, the devil, the day of judgment, a hanged man and the moon are examples. The deck abounds in symbolism and has attracted the interpretations of psychologists as well as occultists.

Survival of Astrology Despite Church Disfavor

Astrology is the most popular occult "science" today and one of the oldest. Some 5,000 years ago Babylonian star-gazers began noting correlations between specific conjunctions of heavenly bodies and favorable or unfavorable turns of events on Earth. They identified 12 groups of stars traversed by the sun and the planets in their wanderings; and they called each group of stars by the name of an animal which its outline

The zodiac: An imaginary measuring device to show relative position of the stars to the Earth, it is divided into 12 equal sections called signs. The signs are divided into 30 degrees apiece, roughly equivalent to lines of longitude and latitude.

The 12 signs: Pisces, Aries, Taurus, Gemini, Cancer, Leo, Virgo, Libra, Scorpio, Sagittarius, Aquarius and Capricorn are grouped into 'quadruplicities' and 'triplicities.'

Signs	Quadruplicities
Aries, Cancer, Libra, Capricorn	Cardinal
Taurus, Leo, Scorpio, Aquarius	Fixed
Gemini, Virgo, Sagittarius, Pisces	Mutable (or Common)

Signs	Triplicities
Aries, Leo, Sagittarius	Fire
Taurus, Virgo, Capricorn	Earth
Gemini, Libra, Aquarius	Air
Cancer, Scorpio, Pisces	Water

If most of the planets are in cardinal signs when a person is born, he is expected by astrologers to be restless, a leader of men and a pioneer, among other things. If the planets also predominate in the triplicities sign of fire, the person will have a stormy temper. An Earth person is dependable; Air people are lively and gay and Water people are sensitive and perhaps overly emotional.

Ephemerides: Astrology tables to place the positions of the Sun, Moon and planets at birth. These tables also show which sign was on the eastern horizon at the place of birth. The point where the eastern horizon appeared to intersect the zodiac is called the 'ascendant' and the sign of the horizon is said to be "on the ascendant." This has an important bearing on personality and destiny.

Houses: Another imaginary division of the sky. The 12 houses represent departments of life, such as personality and appearance (first house) and death (eighth house). Thus the special influence of a planet will operate within an area defined by a house. Combining the attributes of a planet, a sign and a house is the usual method of astrological character analysis. Thus, if Venus (love, affection) in Pisces (watery, mutable) should appear in the fifth house (governing children); an astrologer could conclude that the person could be dreamily impractical about children. It should be noted that astrologers do not agree on the proper method of drawing houses in a horoscope.

Aspects: Positions of planets in relation to other planets. Planets may be "in opposition" or "in conjunction," and these factors will influence an astrologer's analysis. The various angles that planets form in the zodiac also are said to affect personality and fate. Names such as sesquiquadrat, grand trine, sextile and quintile refer to various positionings.

seemed to resemble. The Greeks, adopting the system, called the entire structure the zodiac (circle of animals). (See page 311)

According to tradition the Three Wise Men who visited the new-born babe in Bethlehem were astrologers, forewarned of a momentous event by what they took to be a new star. Centuries later the church condemned astrology. Saint Augustine insisted in *The City of God* that if the predictions of astrologers came true, it was due either to chance or to demons. Pope Sixtus V issued a bull against astrology in 1586, Pope Urban VIII reaffirmed this stand in 1631. Martin Luther had meanwhile concurred in this view. But few paid attention to these pronouncements.

In fact, the ancient Romans had tried unsuccessfully to ban astrology. It began to fall into disfavor, along with many other superstitious beliefs, only late in the 17th century as the Age of Reason began. Nevertheless "a thousand superstitions survived side by side with the rising enlightenment," the Durants noted. Highborn ladies trembled at unfavorable horoscopes; fortunetellers lived on the credit given to their clairvoyance and "Mme. de Pompadour, the Abbe de Bernis and the Duc de Choiseul secretly consulted Mme. Bontemps, who read the future in coffee grounds."[16]

Astrologers divide time into periods of thousands of years. There is no agreement about the dating of these periods—called Great Years—but the 9th and 10th centuries B.C. are generally considered to have been a time of Leo. The approaching age of Aquarius, beginning about the year 2000, replaces the age of Pisces which began about the year 1 A.D.

Relation of Religion with the Occult

CHRISTIANITY HAS BEEN at war with the occult since the Middle Ages for supremacy in the minds of men. The emphasis which preaching laid upon the reality of hell and the wiles of Satan seemed to strengthen popular belief that devils and demons possessed persons and caused them to fall ill, behave oddly, commit crimes and, worse, to cast spells on others. Ac-

---

[16] Will and Ariel Durant, *The Age of Voltaire* (Part IX of *The Story of Civilization*, 1965), p. 493.

cusations of sorcery were made against a great variety of persons, including Pope Boniface VIII (1294-1303). John XXII, during his papacy (1316-1334), ordered the execution of various obscure persons for plotting to kill him by invoking the assistance of demons. Joan of Arc was burned at the stake in 1431 for heresy and sorcery.

Nor did witch hunts abate after the Protestant Reformation. Christians of the 16th century, still believing in demons and hence fearing them, felt an obligation to burn witches. Drawing on the biblical exhortation (Exodus 22:18) "Thou shalt not suffer a witch to live," Luther and Calvin seconded Pope Innocent VIII (1484-92) in urging the persecution of witches. "I would have no compassion on these witches," Luther said. "I would burn them all."[17]

This witch-hunting zeal was soon transmitted across the Atlantic to Puritan New England. A dozen accused witches were hanged in Massachusetts and its neighboring states in the half-century preceding the famous witch trials of 1692 in Salem, Mass. Modern scholarship traces the witchcraft mania in Salem to two young girls—Betty Parris, age 9, and Abigail Williams, age 11, the daughter and niece of the Rev. Samuel Parris of Salem. After listening to tales of witchcraft related by Parris' slave woman Tituba, Betty and Abigail—along with other girls—began exhibiting wildly unusual behavior. Present-day researchers have concluded that the girls found a release in these antics from the strictures of their Puritan faith. They screamed, foamed at the mouth and fell into trances. Parris tried to exorcise them but only made matters worse.

Demanded by their parents to tell who was causing their distress, the girls named Tituba, and neighbors Sarah Good and Sarah Osburne. Many others were subsequently named and a court was convened in June 1692 to try them for witchcraft. Before the year was out, 19 persons were hanged and one man, who refused to testify, Giles Corey, was pressed to death with millstones piled on his chest.

Within a century after the Salem trials belief in witchcraft had withered in Europe and America. The last known execution of an accused witch on the European continent occurred in Switzerland in 1782. But as late as 1765, the most famous of English jurists, Sir William Blackstone, wrote in his *Com-*

---

17 Cited by W.E.H. Lecky, *History of Rationalism,* Vol. II (1910), p. 3.

mentaries: "To deny the possibility, nay, the actual existence, of witchcraft and sorcery is flatly to contradict the revealed word of God...."

Modern Academic Controversy over Witchcraft

There are three currents of thought today about the practice of witchcraft: (1) that it was a delusion; a hoax perpetrated out of superstitious fear and religious zeal; (2) that it was the remnant of some pre-Christian religion that flourished widely throughout Europe; and (3) that it was deliberate worship of the Christian devil, and therefore heresy. The proponents of each theory quote from the same research material yet come to mutually exclusive views.

Rossell Hope Robbins, a specialist in medieval history, is the chief exponent of the witchcraft-as-delusion theory. He contends that witchcraft was "a colossal fraud" perpetrated by inquisitors of the church in persecuting heresy. "An indifferent public was ruthlessly lashed into believing it."—"Never were so many so wrong, so long." [18] Accordingly, witchcraft trials produced rumors of witches, which produced religious hysteria, which produced more trials. Confessions, extracted by torture, kept fear of witchcraft alive.

The view that witchcraft was probably the remnant of an ancient religion was first suggested early in the 20th century by anthropologist Margaret Alice Murray. Her explanation, expanded in *Witch-Cult in Western Europe* (1921), was adopted by the *Encyclopaedia Britannica* and gained a wide acceptance. Those persons who today call themselves witches accept the Murray view—a fact which historian Cavendish described as "an interesting example of life conforming itself to fiction."

Montague Summers, a Roman Catholic priest, is the most famous advocate of the view that witchcraft was heresy, a worship of the devil. Writing in 1926, Summers maintained that a witch was evil—"a social pest and parasite; the devotee of a loathly and obscene creed; an adept at poisoning, blackmail and other creeping crimes; a member of a powerful secret organization inimical to Church and State; a blasphemer in word and deed; swaying the villagers by terror and superstition; a charlatan and a quack sometimes; a bawd; an abortionist; the dark counsellor of lewd court ladies and adul-

---

[18] Rossell Hope Robbins, *The Encyclopedia of Witchcraft and Demonology* (1959), p. 3.

terous gallants; a minister to vice and inconceivable corruption; battening upon the filth and foulest passions of the age."[19] Whatever witchcraft was, was believed to be, or was not, it does represent a black page in history. The *Encyclopedia Americana* ventures the broad estimate that 300,000 to two million persons were executed as witches from 1450 to 1750, the height of the conflict between the churches and the occult.

Revival of 'Evil Cults,' Satanism and Black Mass

Esquire magazine devoted its issue of March 1970 to drug-oriented "evil cults" in California that express themselves in such far-out ways as performing black masses and professing belief in Satanism. The black masses of the Satanists had their beginnings in the witchcraft of the Middle Ages. Basic to Satan worship and the black mass is the idea that the battle between God and the Devil is not yet over, and further that the Devil will win. As it was performed in the Middle Ages—and still is being performed, according to some accounts—the black mass is a parody of Christian Eucharist. Profane rituals are substituted for holy ones. The Lord's Prayer may be recited backwards, with "The Lord of Darkness" praised instead of "God, The Father." In Satanism of an extreme order, the black mass ends in an orgy.

Behavior such as the Satanists might exhibit is on the far fringes of the "new mysticism," of which the drug culture is only one part. Religion is making a bid, albeit haltingly, to recapture those who have turned to the occult for mystical experience. "Rock" masses and religious "happenings" are being staged in many churches to tap the renaissance of spirituality which theologians see in modern society. Harvey Cox, in his book *The Feast of Fools* (1969), suggested that very loud rock music drives a person's consciousness inward and thus may be the equivalent of religious contemplation.

Some seekers of "celebration" and "festivity" in religion profess to find it in Pentecostalism. As practiced for years by some fundamentalist Protestant groups in the United States, it involves speaking in "unknown" tongues and other forms of emotional outbursts, including public confession of sins, shouting with joy and even rolling on the floor in a semi-conscious state. Pentecostalism takes its belief from the Bible's

---

[19] Montague Summers, *op. cit.*, p. xxii.

Book of Acts in which it is recounted that after the resurrection of Jesus the disciples received from the Holy Ghost the gift of speaking in diverse tongues.

For years those who practiced this form of worship were known, derisively, to outsiders as "Holy Rollers." Their churches were likely to be found in the deep recesses of Appalachia or in an abandoned store of a black urban ghetto. Other churches that for years were disdainful of such "excesses" of worship are now saying that perhaps they should reevaluate their own thinking on the matter.

Yet, other Bible scholars hold the fundamentalist tendencies of American Protestantism accountable for the rising popular interest in Eastern religions. "After two millennia of intellectualistic doctrinal disputation, and four centuries of dead-in-earnest Protestant biblical literalism, most of the poetry and all of the flexibility, has gone out of the Christian vocabulary—especially in America, with its superliteralistic, fundamentalist tendencies."[20]

Sensitivity training groups, or "T groups" as they are sometimes known, have sprung up in California and elsewhere to promote self-awareness. Individuals representing a diversity of background and outlook are brought together in an "unstructured" situation under the passive direction of a trained psychologist or psychiatrist. By interacting with each other, members of the group are expected to become aware of their reaction to other people and the reactions of others to them.

Sensitivity training thus is not therapy; its goal is understanding of self. A spokesman for the American Psychiatric Association told Editorial Research Reports he was not surprised that some persons had become interested in the occult through sensitivity training. He suggested that many persons who become involved in these groups are already searching for a greater understanding of themselves and the world. Many of the occult "sciences" offer an explanation of the mysteries of life and thus appeal to these persons. Sensitivity training is widely but not wholeheartedly endorsed by psychologists and psychiatrists. It has come under attack from some of them on grounds that it can worsen mild mental or emotional disorders

---

[20] Winston L. King, "Eastern Religions: A New Interest and Influence." *Annals* (of the American Academy of Political and Social Science), January 1970, p. 67. Dr. King is professor of history of religions at Vanderbilt University.

of the participants if they are not adequately screened beforehand.

Religion writer Edward B. Fiske of *The New York Times* commented that religious leaders "are beginning to conclude that while the churches were becoming more worldly the world was becoming more religious and that the two passed like ships in the night." Fiske said the most obvious sign of a spiritual revival can be seen in increased interest in the occult and Eastern religion and primitive practices such as witchcraft. "For many, it is expressed in the mind-expanding aspects of the drug movement." [21]

Churches' Quest for Relevance in Age of Aquarius

Church spokesmen contend that the church must change as society changes, that it must adapt itself to the new conditions of life and new modes of thought that characterize modern man. The Protestant world is churned up by a radical turn in theological debate in which the very existence of God is brought into question. Catholicism is buffeted by currents of reform unleashed by Vatican Council II. [22] Underlying the problems of both Catholicism and Protestantism, perhaps, is a vague notion among many people that religion has lost its meaning and influence. Gallup polls tend to bear out this thought, at least in the United States. Of the American adults interviewed by the polling organization in 1957, only 14 per cent said they thought organized religion was losing influence; by 1965 this number had climbed to 45 per cent, and in 1970 to 75 per cent. Moreover, churches are beginning to experience difficulty filling clerical ranks. The official *Catholic Directory* recorded a 5.6 per cent decrease between 1966 and 1969 in the number of priests, nuns and others in religious orders. In that time, the American Catholic population increased by about 3.5 per cent. A number of Protestant seminaries have reported declining enrollments and headquarters of several denominations have been forced by economic necessity to reduce the size of their staffs.

The proportion of American adults who belong to churches has declined steadily since 1958, when a peak figure of 68 per cent was recorded. As indicated by a Gallup poll published in

21 Edward B. Fiske, "Uncertainty in Church," *The New York Times,* April 11, 1970.

22 The Second Vatican Council opened Oct. 11, 1962, in Rome, met for several months in the autumn of four successive years, and held its final session Dec. 8, 1965. See "Religion in Upheaval," *E.R.R.,* 1967 Vol. I, pp. 3-19.

March 1970, the figure had since declined to 63 per cent. Church records tend to confirm a lag in both membership and attendance in terms of population growth.

Declining membership and attendance alone may not reveal the true dimensions of what theologians now call the "crisis" of organized religions. Many have accepted the premise Will Herberg advanced in 1955, that a vast number of Americans equate church-going with civic duty rather than religious conviction. In his book *Protestant-Catholic-Jew* (1955), Herberg wrote of this country's patriotic "civil religion."

Science, which for two centuries or more has replaced the occult as the gravest challenge to religion, is not benefitting from the current disenchantment with churches. The young, especially, hold science to account for at least as many wrongs in society as they do organized religion. [23] For the immediate future, it is unlikely that either science or religion will be able to loosen the grip of occultism on the minds of millions of Americans. Whether popular interest in the occult becomes a lasting thing, however, depends on how well religion and science respond to their detractors.

---

[23] See "Science and Society," *E.R.R.*, 1969 Vol. II, pp. 775-791.

Communal Living

by

Helen B. Shaffer

1 9 6 9
Aug. 6

COMMUNAL LIVING

THE COMMUNAL LIVING movement, which spawned scores of little utopias from Maine to California during the 19th century, is having a curious revival in the troubled late 1960s. Even more remarkable are indications that certain aspects of the communal living idea may be taking root at last in American society.

Communal living can take a number of forms, but one principle is basic: the individual works solely for the good of the group and all share alike in the proceeds of one another's work. Paradoxically, dedication to the common good is expected to be a boon to the individual. Not only is he to be assured the necessities of life from cradle to grave but, freed from the pressures of a competitive society, his personality may be expected to flower and his inborn creativity to find full expression. The hoped-for result is the creation of a social order in which men will live together in peace and harmony.

Many attempts at creating communal sub-societies have been made in the past. All, at least in the western world, either have failed or have survived as isolated enclaves, sheltered from contaminating influences of the main society. Today, however, a number of small communes have come into existence in cities as close neighbors of traditionally organized family units, and it is beginning to appear that a broadened base of family sharing (which is, in effect, what communal living consists of) may someday become a generally accepted part of the American style of life.

To the average American, firmly attached to the principle of private ownership—of his house, his car, his bank account —the idea of communal living is outrageous. The very sound of the words conjures up images of police-state oppression, "free love," "group sex" or crackpot reformism. Most Americans obviously want nothing to do with communal living, even in its most benign coloration, and they are not likely to change their minds in the near future.

But the prevailing hostility toward communal living and toward those who adopt this mode of existence is not necessarily permanent. If there is one thing certain in the contemporary world, it is that times change: technology moves ahead and as it moves the mechanics of daily living and the attitudes of people toward social forms may undergo rapid change. What once seemed incontrovertible about the nature of the good life in America or about the proper relationships between individuals is now being questioned. New value concepts are being adopted by more and more persons. Quickest to accept new criteria pertaining to morals and manners are the young, the fad-setters of today and the social controllers of tomorrow. And it is among the young that communal living is being accepted, not necessarily as the appropriate norm for American life but as quite all right for those who want to live that way.

A number of young Americans, seeking a more humanly satisfying life than the one conventionally available to them, have adopted the communal living pattern. While their number is not large, it appears to be growing. If the movement persists and spreads, some form of communal living may well become a familiar element rather than an oddity in the social structure of the nation. In that event, it might ultimately come to be widely viewed as a worthy alternative to the standard by which each family ("mom-pop and the kids") lives, earns and spends as an exclusive social and economic unit.

Hippie Sharing of Food, Clothing and Shelter

The most publicized manner of communal living on the American scene today is associated with the hippie movement. Communal living flowered naturally from the hippie's philosophy of life: his rejection of the middle-class work ethic, his contempt for money and personal property, his belief in the socially regenerative power of love. As voluntary outcasts from the main society, choosing to live hand-to-mouth, hippies have had a practical as well as philosophic reason for falling into a style of living in which food, clothing, "pad" and "pot" are shared in a hippie "family."

How many young Americans have become converted to the hippie's communal living plan can hardly be estimated, any more than one can count the total number of true hippies in the country. The movement, which emerged in the mid-

1960s as an identifiable segment of the youth revolt, is believed to have passed its peak in 1967 or 1968 when "perhaps 200,000 people grooved on their new freedom and on each other." [1] But many of those who flocked to the Haight-Ashbury section of San Francisco, to the East Village in New York, or to other hippie-concentration areas of big cities were not true converts to the movement but simply restless adolescents, still leashed to conventional homes, who enjoyed acting out the hippie role for a while. Of those who became submerged in the hippie community, some moved in with fellow "cop-outs" in whatever housing was available and pooled their meager resources to pay rent and buy food.

Much of this kind of communal living was casual. Most of those who drifted in and out of the communal pads probably thought of them not in terms of a social concept, but simply as places where the living was free and the individual could do as he chose. The philosophers of the hippie movement,[2] however, did not view communal living as a convenience or an economic necessity; they considered it an inherent element of a new society based on peace, individual liberty, and the brotherhood of man.

An "over-30" apologist for the movement wrote in an underground newspaper two years ago: "There is [among hippies] an incredible seeking out, testing & creation of new forms of living together and of raising children: meditation, communal living, tribalization. . . . There are new economic forms being contemplated, a new 'primitive' communism. . . . There is a rebirth of communal work, even in the egotistic arts." [3] Allen Ginsberg, the beatnik poet of the 1950s who became a hippie guru in the 1960s, has drawn a vision of a future when Americans will be united in a peace-loving brotherhood: "Likely an enlarged family unit will emerge for many citizens, possibly . . . with matrilineal descent as courtesy to those . . . whose . . . holy path is the sexual liberation. . . . Children may be held in common." [4]

Use of drugs doubtless contributed to the evolution of the hippie's communal life style. As a shared act of defiance

---

[1] Jesse Kornbluth, "The Hippies: Flowering of a Non-Movement," Jesse Kornbluth, ed., *Notes From the Underground* (1968), p. 200.

[2] An essential feature of the hippie ethos is that there are no "leaders" of the movement but that poets and philosophers may speak for it.

[3] Tuli Kupferberg, "The Hip and the Square: The Hippie Generation" (reprinted from *Berkeley Barb*, Aug. 4, 1967) in Jesse Kornbluth, ed., *op. cit.*, p. 207.

[4] Allen Ginsberg, "Renaissance or Die" (reprinted from *The East Village Other*, Jan. 10, 1967) in Jesse Kornbluth, ed., *op. cit.*, pp. 56-57.

against the laws of the main society, the taking of drugs fostered the sense of community among sharers of the same pad, and the drugs themselves apparently had the effect on some users of fortifying that sense. "Drugs break patterns. . . . When patterns are broken, new worlds can emerge," a pro-hippie poet wrote.[5] "Whether or not they have found God, as many claim," said a more objective observer, "there do seem to be important changes in values associated with the taking of these drugs."[6] However, some of the hippie communes ban drug-taking, if only to ward off police raids.

Operation of Stores and Hostels by 'Diggers'

In the early autumn of 1967, the proprietors of the Psychedelic Shop in Haight-Ashbury, out of funds and behind in their rent, closed their shop and sent out invitations to a funeral for "Hippie, devoted son of Mass Media." The mock service was held in a public park at sunrise, Oct. 6, 1967. The point of the ceremony was to emphasize, not that the movement for a new way of life was dead, but that its true believers were through with the word "hippie." This was because it had come to mean to them a distortion of an idealistic search for a better way of life than that offered by a society which they rejected as commercial, war-making, dehumanized. They were through with commercialization of hippie fashions and bric-a-brac, with "plastic hippies" (kids who merely dressed the part and hung around for kicks), and with tourists to whom hippieland was just another sideshow.

There remained a hard core whose alienation from the main society and whose dedication to the communal life was genuine and was based on at least an embryonic philosophy of life. Among these were the Diggers, known to some as the saints of the hippie movement, who had operated free stores, food stations and hostels in the hippie communities. The Diggers took their name from one of the egalitarian bands of 17th century England whose members appropriated land, cultivated it, and gave away the food produced.

Like their predecessors, the latter-day Diggers are opposed

---

[5] Tuli Kupferberg, *op. cit.*, p. 208. The favored drugs are marijuana, which hippies consider harmless, and, to a lesser extent, LSD. They realize that LSD may give some users a "bad trip," but they nevertheless consider it desirable as a mind and sensibility stretcher. Reports on hippie culture tend to agree that hard addictive drugs—opium and heroin—are not approved. Use of Methedrine, a powerful amphetamine known as "Speed," declined when its dangers were recognized; hippies now warn that " 'Speed' kills."

[6] Gerald Dworkin, "The Hippies: Permanent Revolution?" *Dissent*, March/April 1969, p. 180.

to the use of money, believing that everything needed to feed man's body and soul should be produced without pay to the producers and distributed without cost to those who need it. To maintain their free stores and soup kitchens, the Diggers begged and scrounged for the food they dispensed without charge. They accepted gifts of food and goods but not money. "They repudiated the cash nexus and sought to relate to people in terms of their needs," according to one report.[7] "They will burn your ten dollar bill if you offer it," reported another.[8]

Movement of "Freemen" to Country Communes

The Diggers' enterprises are less visible in the cities today than they were a year or two ago but the Digger spirit continues to motivate the remnants of what were called hippies. And the name they now prefer is "freeman." Many "freemen" have left the city and taken to the hills or the backwoods, where they hope to establish new communities beyond reach of unfriendly police, marauding thugs and the "plastic hippies." It has been reported, for example, that hundreds, possibly 1,000 "flower children" have become owners of land in mountain areas of northern New Mexico, where they have taken up residence in abandoned adobe houses and tepees. A realtor in Taos, N.M., estimated the value of their combined land purchases at $500,000, evidence that the flower children still have some claim on the affluence of their middle-class origins.

Other accounts describe communes in wilderness or rural settings in Arizona, New York, New England, Oregon and in California, where the Big Sur area has attracted former denizens of urban hippieland. "In a few years, there'll be a whole network of communes from coast to coast—like Howard Johnsons," predicted an optimistic member of a communal family that had moved from a southern California hillside to an abandoned Pennsylvania farm and was trying to reassemble again in California.[9]

Dr. David E. Smith of the University of California Medical School, who once directed a free clinic in Haight-Ashbury, told a doctors' meeting in San Francisco, April 10,

---

[7] John Robert Howard, "The Flowering of the Hippie Movement," *Annals of the American Academy of Political and Social Science*, March 1969, p. 46.

[8] Ralph J. Gleason, "The Power of Non-Politics or the Death of the Square Left" (reprinted from *Evergreen Review*, September 1967) in Jesse Kornbluth, ed., *op. cit.*, p. 218.

[9] Robert Houriet, "Life and Death of a Commune Called Oz," *New York Times Magazine*, Feb. 16, 1969, p. 31.

that it was a mistake to believe the hippie movement was dead simply because so many had deserted Haight-Ashbury, which had now become a "violent teen-age ghetto." He said: "The hippie movement has greatly increased but is now redirected and redistricted into rural and urban communes." The flower children were trying to "fade out of the media limelight" in order to discourage invasion of their retreats by outsiders. Dr. Smith and an associate had visited rural communes where serious efforts were under way to create functioning, self-contained communities in which the expanded "freeman" family could live and raise children in accordance with their beliefs.

Dr. Smith described communes held together by a mystic sense of brotherhood and reverence for life. Many members, he reported, will eat no meat. There is marriage within the communes but not necessarily with benefit of marriage certificate. Strangely, in view of the prominence of drugs in hippie culture, the women take no drugs during pregnancy and insist on natural childbirth.[10] Births may not be registered. "If there are no birth certificates," Dr. Smith said, "there will be no Social Security numbers" and the child will presumably be "safe from the draft." He urged a greater effort to understand the stresses that alienate these young people, many of whom are former students or graduates of high-ranking colleges and universities. Otherwise, he warned, "More and more of our children will move into psychedelic communes."

Walden II Community; Urban Communal Living

The hippie or "freeman" movement does not by any means embrace the entirety of the communal living movement today. Some communes springing up in city and country are more closely related to the world as it is rather than as the hippie would like it to be. But the hippie movement put the spotlight on the growth of communal living, brought to mind again the utopian brotherhood experiments of the past, and influenced many young Americans outside the hippie movement to look favorably on the communal ideal. Some of them are now quietly trying to live by it without recourse to beads, bells, or mystic incantations.

---

[10] Muffyn, a young wife and member of a temporarily disbanded rural commune, has described the difficulty she and her long-haired husband had in New York finding a doctor "who would do natural childbirth as it was our first and therefore we didn't want to deliver it ourselves."—Letter in *New York Times Magazine*, March 9, 1969, p. 14.

Communal Living

Unique among contemporary efforts to create a viable communal society is Twin Oaks, a 123-acre farm in Louisa County, Virginia, purchased in June 1967 by the eight founders of the community. Membership now totals 16, including several children, and more families are expected to join shortly. Twin Oaks is frankly an "experiment in living," constituting an effort to test the validity of the fictional utopia described 20 years ago by the Harvard psychologist B. F. Skinner [11] in his novel *Walden II*. Twin Oaks advertises for recruits, hoping that at least 1,000 will ultimately be willing to try a way of life that promises, in the words of its prospectus, "no rules to enforce, no personal competition, no money to be misused, and no glory or power to be gained by any single individual."

Twin Oaks life is poor by outside standards, but the colony by no means glorifies poverty. A major objective is to become so efficient in production that members will be able to live well and yet have leisure to pursue satisfying personal activities. The colony supports itself by growing wheat and garden vegetables and by raising cattle; it also manufactures rope hammocks which it markets to the public. When funds run short, members take outside jobs but as soon as the community becomes solvent again, the job holders are recalled. All earnings are pooled and distribution of goods, including clothes is communal.

New currents in Christian theology, stressing the mission of religion in the secular world, have helped to provide the philosophic basis for communal living arrangements. Antiwar activism and involvement in the crisis of the cities among clergy and lay members of both Catholic and Protestant denominations have been unifying factors in some communal groups. The 200 members of the faculty and research staff of the Ecumenical Institute in Chicago live together communally in a former seminary.[12] "Bound together under a common covenant," an Institute leaflet states, "the faculty is an experimental 'family order' discovering

[11] Known also for his creation of the "teaching machine" or the process of "programed learning," and for his invention of the Skinner Box in which infants may be kept without clothing in an ideal physical environment. Dr. Skinner had no part in the founding of Twin Oaks.

[12] The Ecumenical Institute, founded in accordance with a 1954 resolution of the World Council of Churches, is essentially a new-style missionary society, dedicated to carrying out a comprehensive program for "reformulation" of urban civilization. One of its activities is a special project in a Chicago ghetto designed to draw all residents into participation in community-regeneration activities. It is hoped that this project will become a model for remaking cities the world over.

what it means to be a disciplined body of people for the sake of the mission of the church." Some of the members hold salaried jobs outside the mission, but all contribute their earnings to it. The communal family includes married couples and their children as well as single persons. Among its research goals are the development of new "procedures for the training of adults, youth and children" and the testing of "new models of the family." The Ecumenical Institute has branched out to other cities—Atlanta, Boston, Rockford, Ill., and Washington, D.C., among them—and to a number of places overseas.

Perhaps the nearest thing to a "wave of the future" in communal living is the small group that shares a house or an apartment in the city. This new-style commune rarely has more than 15 members and usually includes at least several couples. Some are former hippies, some are political radicals, and some are simply individuals seeking a happier life in an enlarged family of like-minded persons. No one knows how many communes of this type there are, but the number in large cities, including an estimated 40 to 60 in Washington, D.C., is believed to be growing.

For the most part, these communes represent a phase of the youth revolt against the manner of life of the older generation. Sexual freedom has played a part in growth of the communes, as has the trend away from campus living by university students. Joint activity in a particular project, ranging from political protest to running a puppet theater, may be the original unifying factor. In an article on the newer communes, the *New York Times*, Aug. 2, 1969, cited a six-house commune in Boston whose members own a corporation that produces films and records and publishes a magazine. The essence of the commune, however, is that the members constitute a single family, pooling their resources, sharing their provender.

Small communes of this kind, formed by students or young adults, are not peculiar to the United States. They have had perhaps their greatest growth in West Berlin, where estimates of the number range from 40 to 150, and they have been spreading in the Federal Republic of Germany, in northern Italy, and in the Scandinavian countries. Some of the communes are in effect cells of radical activity. But the major motive appears to be the search for a new way of life, one in which troubled young people can shed their individualistic "hangups" and possibly transform society.

Communes in Other Places and Times

THE RECORD of man's experience in living as a member of a genuinely communal society is one of many attempts and almost as many failures. Even in Communist countries, where the basic ideology extols common ownership of the means of production and of the goods produced, communal living in its pure form has not taken root. In Soviet Russia it is officially discouraged.

Immediately after the Russian revolution, many communes were formed, but their number soon declined and, following a brief resurgence a decade later during the period of farm collectivization, they passed out of the Soviet picture. Stalin in 1930 called a halt to formation of new rural communes and ordered existing ones to be converted into artels, a form of collective in which the means of agricultural production are held in common and members farm jointly but each household is a separate consuming unit and owns its own garden plot and livestock. Official displeasure was directed also to dozens of urban and factory workers' communes that sprang up in the 1929-1931 period.

"The acme of the [Russian] Revolution was the commune," writes an historian of the movement. ". . . In it, as nowhere else, the ideals of the Revolution were incarnated: brotherly living and working together in equality and sharing all things freely without greed or envy, as in the communal societies dreamed by utopians of all times." [13] But the communes formed by young enthusiasts inspired by the share-alike ideal did not satisfy the practical needs of the Soviet regime. The communes were encouraged for a time, for they served as models of idealism and mutual benefit. Then they were criticized for being geared to maximizing consumption by commune members rather than to producing for the good of the nation.

> The Soviet authorities wanted the collective farms to sell as much as possible to the government to feed the cities and, through exports, help finance the industrialization of the country. . . . But communes were . . . prone to consume their own produce. . . . [The commune's] usefulness came to an end when the mass of peasants was collectivized and direct party controls were established in the countryside.

[13] Robert G. Wesson, *Soviet Communes* (1963), p. 3. See also "Soviet Agriculture: Record of Stagnation," *E.R.R.*, 1964 Vol. I, pp. 71-76.

. . . It was an economic failure from the point of view of the state, since it tended to defeat the main purpose of collectivization, the procurement of maximum amounts of grain from the peasants.[14]

Communist China in 1958 launched a major program of reorganization that made the rural commune the basic administrative, economic and social unit of the nation. Some 750,000 agricultural cooperatives were regrouped into 26,000 communes, each containing 3,000-5,000 households. The plan called for a major step-up in agricultural production, development of industry within the communes, and political education of the masses.

The life of the Chinese peasant was forcibly altered. He gave up his land to the commune, his children were placed in public nurseries or boarding schools, his wife was inducted into the full-time labor force, and he began to take his meals with fellow workers in large mess halls. Piecework pay was abolished as a relic of bourgeois decadence. Workers were paid partly in goods, with the understanding that, as the commune became able to do so, it would compensate them increasingly in the form of goods and services rather than cash.[15] Failure to meet production goals in 1959 and 1960 led to a retreat from the commune ideal; incentive pay was restored and peasants were permitted to cultivate private plots and market their produce independently.

The large-scale commune is apparently still the goal in Red China. Government propaganda occasionally refers to the voluntary return of private plots to the communes, but there is no indication that this is widespread. The *Far Eastern Economic Review* noted that the 10th anniversary of the founding of the communes passed without fanfare, commenting that "The answer presumably lies in the fact that even China's most radical leaders have pragmatism forced upon them when they think of feeding the 700 million." [16] The Peking government in June 1969 invited foreign journalists to visit a 6,400-acre commune of 40,000 population in the western hills; those who did so noted that the communal kitchens and dining halls had not been reinstated and that peasants were growing produce for their own use on private plots.

---

[14] Robert G. Wesson, *op. cit.*, pp. 225-226, 232-235.

[15] Some of the more prosperous communes actually provided not only free food, clothing, housing and education, but also extras like free haircuts, baths, movies, and wedding and funeral services.—Gargi Dutt, *Rural Communes of China* (1967), pp. 40-42. See also "Red China's Communes," *E.R.R.*, 1959 Vol. I, pp. 205-222.

[16] Colina MacDougall, "Just a Change of Name?" *Far Eastern Economic Review*, Sept. 26, 1968, p. 608.

Communal Living

True communal living is purely voluntary and owes little to the example of the Communist countries. Its origins lie chiefly in Christian sectarianism and secular utopianism, both of which were given short shrift by theorists of the Communist revolutions.[17] The belief that man can live a more beautiful or more holy life in a communal rather than a competitive social order has been traced to the early Greek myth of a "golden age," believed to have existed in a dim past when men lived as nature intended, in peace and as brotherly equals, holding property in common. Plato in *The Republic* described an ideal state as one in which all property was collectivized among the ruling aristocracy. Sir Thomas More carried on the communal property concept of an ideal world in *Utopia,* published in 1516.

Early Communes in the American Hinterland

The early church fathers adapted the golden-age myth to Christian theology. The monastic orders, beginning with the Benedictines in the sixth century, practiced communal living. "By the late medieval period, Christian scholars had accepted as a fact the teaching that the early Christians had rejected private property and that this rejection . . . brought man closer to God."[18] The Reformation set loose forces that produced numerous sects whose members were determined to live as they believed the original Christians did, that is, communally.[19] The earliest communal colonies in the United States were formed by members of such sects, who sought refuge from persecution plus an opportunity to create a godly life in the distant wilderness. From the 17th through the 19th century they came—Anabaptists, Separatists, Moravians and members of other small sects in defiance of the established churches in their homelands.

> For the first century and a half of its history in America, the communitarian point of view was peculiarly associated with religion. Its ultimate origin is to be found in the idea . . . that believers constitute a separate and consecrated body set over against the sinful world—a Chosen People as the Hebrews phrased it, a City of God in the language of St. Augustine. . . . Such a separation from the world is thought to afford not only a means to individual salvation but also an example of the life through which all men may be redeemed.[20]

---

[17] Karl Marx rejected the many communal colonies that existed in his day as ineffective instruments for remaking the larger society. One reason for lack of enthusiasm for the communes that appeared in Russia after the revolution was that Soviet leaders tended to associate them with the forms of primitive communism practiced by various Christian sects in pre-revolutionary Russia.

[18] John W. Bennett, *Hutterian Brethren* (1967), p. 39.

[19] Acts 3, 44, 45 of the New Testament provided the justification: "And all that believed were together, and had all things common; And sold their possessions and goods, and parted them to all men, as every man had need."

[20] Arthur Eugene Bestor Jr., *Backwoods Utopias* (1950), p. 4.

The first communal settlement in the New World was short-lived: a Dutch Mennonite colony founded in 1663 on the Delaware River, which was overrun the next year by the British. The most successful of the early ventures was that of the Shakers (United Society of Believers), a group originating in England that established its first American community in 1776 at Watervliet, N.Y., then a thickly wooded wilderness. The Shaker colony possessed some of the characteristics of a cloistered religious order: there were grades of membership, the select were celibate, and men and women worked, ate, and worshiped separately. The outside world, however, was impressed by the prospering of the community's simple economy, based largely on gardening, preserving, and crafts. The Shakers attracted new converts and additional colonies were founded in New England and the Middle West, some continuing to exist as distinct communities into the 20th century.

Another unusually long-lived, religion-based communal enterprise was that of the Society of True Inspiration, a German sect that first settled in 1843 near Buffalo, then moved to a 25 000-acre tract in Iowa where it established Amana (meaning "Believe faithfully"), which grew into a community of seven inter-related villages. Here again an industrious, resourceful, and thrifty people succeeded in providing a comfortable and satisfying life without paying wages or depending on outside support. Their agriculture-crafts-small industry economy flourished on a communal basis until 1932 when, pressed by loss of markets due to the depression and no longer so strong in fidelity to the communal idea, the remaining members voted to convert the enterprise into a profit-sharing corporation; qualified members of the old communal order became stockholders of the new Amana. A decade ago, a visitor who had been raised in one of the villages, wrote that "With each visit, it seems that less and less remains of the old communities." [21]

Short-Lived Experiments of Secular Utopians

Early in the 19th century, the communitarian movement in the United States received a new infusion of energy from the preachments of secular reformers who sought to promote the establishment of communal settlements not to save men's souls but to demonstrate the possibilities of a more heavenly

---

[21] Barbara S. Yambura and Eunice Bodine, *A Change and a Parting: My Story of Amana* (1960), p. 351.

life on earth. The philosophy of Jean Jacques Rousseau, who held that man was naturally good but was made evil by the harsh society in which he lives, was influential in providing the rationale for the secular utopian movement. Two other European theorists of social reform—the Welshman Robert Owen and the Frenchman Charles Fourier—were directly responsible for both the popularization of the communal movement and the actual founding of communal colonies in the United States.

In 1825, Owen, whose experiments in factory reform had won him international fame, purchased a 30,000-acre property in Indiana which was being vacated by one of the German-origin communal sects.[22] Owen named the site New Harmonie and invited "the well-disposed and industrious of all nations" to join in an experiment in pure communism, in which all labor would have equal value and all would be provided with whatever was needed for the good life. New Harmonie is the communitarian movement's most famous failure. Owen lost most of his fortune on the experiment, which fell apart in 1828, a disaster that also befell nearly a dozen sister communities.

About 15 years later there was another surge of communal activity, many of the new settlements being based on the more definitely structured plans devised by Fourier. Conversion of Horace Greeley and Albert Brisbane of the *New York Tribune* to the Fourier brand of socialism helped to popularize his plan for communal living. Between 1841 and 1860 at least 28 so-called Fourier Phalanxes (the term he used to designate economic units of a communal enterprise) were established in Illinois, Indiana, Iowa, Massachusetts, New Jersey, New York, Ohio, Pennsylvania, Texas and Wisconsin. The famous Brook Farm colony (1841-1847), founded by New England literati near Boston, went through a Fourierist phase. None lasted out the century.

Other colonies of various secular or religious inspiration were founded, and there was much visiting back and forth and interchange of influence among them. Possibly the best known was Oneida Community in Madison County, N.Y., founded in 1848 by the Perfectionist sect, whose leader, John Humphrey Noyes, wrote one of the early histories of the

---

[22] This had been the community of the Harmonists, led by George Rapp from Wurttemberg, who moved his group in 1824 to Economy, Pa., where it flourished until it became rent with internal disputes toward the end of the century. The Harmonists' Pennsylvania land was sold off and the communality dissolved in 1903.

movement. Noyes described the movement as "a hope watching for the morning in thousands and perhaps millions . . . [of] socialists without theory—believers in the possibility of scientific and heavenly reconstruction of society."[23] An oddity of this colony was "complex marriage," a system of community-controlled mating designed to effect genetic improvement of the population. The community lost its communal character in 1879.

The secular colonies were less durable than the sectarian, being open to motley and hence divisive membership and lacking the sectarians' strong bond of piety and obeisance to authority. One of the more enduring was Icaria, founded by the French author and publicist, Etienne Cabet, whose followers sought to recreate the manner of living he described in his enormously popular novel *Un Voyage en Icarie*, published in 1840. Factionalism developed at the colony in Nauvoo, Ill., and it was liquidated in 1895.

Reformist Influences in 19th Century Communes

Records show that 178 utopian communities were established in the United States during the 19th century, but the actual number is believed to have been much larger. They tended to locate west of the Mississippi after mid-century. California became a favored destination for communal-minded visionaries whose recruitment of followers was inadvertently aided by advertisements, placed by railroads and chambers of commerce, boasting of California's climate.

The inspiration for the latter-day utopias was multiple: transcendentalism, socialism, vegetarianism, the abolitionist movement, women's rights all played a part. The communal movement reflected the rising revulsion against the social penalties of industrialization. Henry George's promotion of the single tax and Edward Bellamy's concept of a nationalized cooperative economy were influential. The early labor movement, with its emphasis on mutual aid and sickness and death benefits, helped to create a sympathetic constituency for experiments that promised lifetime security from want. And there were new religion-based colonies, often of an exotic character. The Theosophical Society, whose doctrines combined humanitarianism with delvings into the occult, founded a number of communal colonies in the West.[24] The later experiments were no more lasting than the earlier.

---

[23] John Humphrey Noyes, *History of American Socialism* (1870), p. 24.
[24] Robert V. Hine, *California's Utopian Colonies* (1953), pp. 160-165.

Outlook for Success of New Communes

PAST ATTEMPTS to create a voluntary communal social order offer much to support the view that man is inherently acquisitive and competitive and hence can never—save in special circumstances—be content to live for long on a purely communal basis. Only two major communal groups exist today that seriously challenge this cynical view—the Hutterite colonies in western Canada and the United States and the kibbutzim (collective settlements) in Israel. The former constitute a religiously united, secluded community with a way of life little changed from that of its founding fathers in 16th century Germany. The latter is a totally secular, 20th century enterprise which, rather than isolating itself from the larger state, has been a major contributor to its ideology and leadership.

Despite their differences of motivation, the two are similar in the completeness of their communal organization. Both are rugged agricultural societies, inhospitable to vanities of dress or decor. Both have an egalitarian social and political structure; provide all members with cradle-to-grave security but pay no wages; maintain communal kitchens and mess halls; and depend more on community approval or disapproval than on police-court action to discipline offenders.

In both, education of the young to the communal ideal is of paramount importance. As expected, both are endlessly fascinating to psychologists and sociologists as living laboratories of the effect of child-rearing in a communal society as a conditioner of human behavior.[25]

Lessons From the Hutterites and From Israel

The Hutterites[26] came to the United States during the 1870s from the Russian Ukraine, where they had settled a century earlier following a series of flights from persecution in other parts of eastern Europe. Like the kibbutz founders, the 100 Hutterite families who migrated to Dakota Territory in 1874 faced a formidable task of pioneering and,

---

[25] The most recent book on this theme is Bruno Bettelheim's *Children of the Dream* (1969), which deals with the children of the Israeli kibbutz.

[26] The Hutterites take their name from Jacob Hutter, Anabaptist minister from the Tyrol, who preached pacifism and communal ownership of property. He was burned for heresy in 1536.

again like the Israeli pioneers, their extraordinary indus-
triousness and their commitment to the communal under-
taking proved almost miraculously productive. When the
Hutterites ran afoul of American draft laws in 1917,[27] most
of them moved on to new pioneer settlements in western
Canada. One reason for the Hutterites' success is that,
though they sought to bar worldly influences on the faith
and customs of their community, they were highly receptive
to introduction of modern farm machinery and methods.

The originators of the kibbutzim were a far cry from the
pietistic Hutterites, though the former also hailed from a
persecuted religious minority group in eastern Europe.
Those who established the first kibbutz in Israel in 1908[28]
were impelled not by a dream of a perfect society nor by the
hope of salvation, but by a passion to build a Jewish home-
land. This desire was compounded by their youthful rebel-
lion against the manner of life of their parents. Pioneer
agriculture, demanding physical labor under hardship conditions, appealed strongly to young intellectuals scornful
both of the narrow religiosity and the petty trader occupations of the ghetto Jew.[29] The communal organization of the
kibbutz "did not arise . . . in response to any preconceived
plan, as did the various utopian societies" in other lands.

> The first kibbutz . . . was formed, initially, as a temporary ex-
> periment, an alternative to the Zionist settlement policy of admin-
> istering farms through an appointed manager, with hired Jewish
> labor. The success of the collective from the outset led to a more
> permanent arrangement. As time went on, the patterns of organiza-
> tion and of an ideology evolved, and by the latter part of the 1920s
> the basic structure of the modern Israeli collective had crystallized.[30]

While both Hutterite and kibbutz experience have much
to teach about the techniques of successful communal living,
it is doubtful if either could serve as a model for the newer
types of communes appearing on the American scene. Communality survives among the Hutterites largely because the
communal community is in fact their church and because
their religion requires that they live "separate from the

[27] Patriotic fervor during World War I turned against the pacifist, German-speaking
Hutterites. Imprisonment of their young men as draft-dodgers led to the move to
Canada, where they were promised a haven in unsettled lands in the West.

[28] A generation earlier, young European Jews, spurred by pogroms that followed
the assassination in 1881 of Czar Alexander II, had tried to establish a pioneer agricultural community in Palestine, but the supporting organization in Russia fell away,
many of the pioneers died, and the project collapsed.

[29] Boris Stern, *The Kibbutz That Was* (1965), p. 6.

[30] Eliyahu Kanovsky, *The Economy of the Israeli Kibbutz* (Harvard Middle Eastern
Monographs XIII, 1966), pp. 3, 126.

world." The danger of alien elements entering the community is small; although open to converts, few outsiders care to join them and the Hutterites do not proselytize.[31]

Hutterite Land Acquisition; Pause for Kibbutzim

It is Hutterite practice that when a communal colony, known as a Bruederhof, reaches a population of around 150, some of its members split off and form another colony on a new tract. In this way the Hutterites have spread over approximately 170 colonies, the older ones occupying 4,000-6,000 acres. Though Hutterites are known as good neighbors, their efforts to buy large tracts of land for new colonies have met resistance and there has been legislation in several Canadian provinces limiting their land purchases.[32] Even if there were not this resistance, the Hutterites would be having difficulty finding sufficient suitable property. "For over 400 years [they] have sought underpopulated frontier areas for their settlement. Now there are few available frontiers."[33]

Opinions differ on the longevity of the communal life of the kibbutz. The communities retain high prestige in Israel but, despite efforts to recruit members from the outside, the kibbutz population has not grown significantly in the past decade; the number stands now at 83,000 living in 233 kibbutzim. In the larger colonies, some of the earlier features of communal life have been modified. For example, the communal showers which once "provided a popular forum for discussion on world affairs, an outlet for local gossip and for expression of personal gripes," have been replaced by private facilities. And limited-membership social clubs, once denounced as anti-communal in spirit and as "an attempt to bring the decadent cafe life of the city to the kibbutz," have become more common.[34] But the essential features of the true commune are firmly entrenched, and respect for the colonies remains high in the nation.

---

[31] So successful were the Hutterites in keeping out the world that few except their nearest neighbors were aware of them until a few decades ago. A history of the communal movement, published in 1941 (V. F. Calverton's *Where Angels Dared to Tread*), did not mention them.

[32] Local prejudice arises out of fear that large land acquisitions by the sect speed the disappearance of small family farms. There is also resentment because the Hutterites take no part in civil affairs outside their own communities, and they buy supplies wholesale in cities rather than buying from nearby retailers.—Victor Peters, *All Things Common: The Hutterian Way of Life* (1965), pp. 51-71.

[33] Paul K. Conkin, *Two Paths to Utopia* (1964), p. 99.

[34] Boris Stern, *op. cit.*, pp. 140-141.

Whether the communes being established in the United States today can achieve as much stability as the two foregoing prime examples of communal success is questionable. The hippie communes in the back country seem to offer mere interludes of primitive tribalism, romantically appealing to city-bred youth, rather than the beginnings of viable social and economic communities. Daniel B. Reibel, curator of Old Economy Village at Ambridge, Pa., the remains of the Harmonists' communal 19th century settlement, recently observed that the hippie communes lacked what he considered the four essentials of commune success: (1) a large enough financial base so that no help would be needed from outside; (2) restriction of membership to all except those who fully subscribe to the goals of the group; (3) strong leadership; and (4) a definite job or function for each member of the community.[35] Experience in the wilderness has apparently taught some hippie communes to modify their antipathy to organization, at least to the extent of working out a job assignment plan. A "working anarchy" is the way one communard described his tribal system.

New Communes as Pointers to Change in Values

Whether or not any of these communal colonies, farms or houses survive may not be so important as the question of what they may foretell of a future way of looking at life, family and society. It has been asserted that "much of the impetus for change in social values" originates in the "underculture" and that middle-class America in fact hungrily absorbs its arts, its fashions, its thought and even its "moral passions" from its rebels.

> The rebellious attempts at tribal life contain a relevant protest against a widely painful and perhaps unviable social form: the small, competitive suburban family. . . . Efforts toward broader families, now endemic in marginal groups, may often be poignant or messy, but they . . . may forecast the crucial community sense of the future.[36]

The communal family may seem to some to be the alternative to the high divorce rate and the psychiatrist's couch. It may be seen also as the beginning of the end of the ideal of privacy as an essential of the good life. Loss of privacy remains the biggest obstacle to acceptance of communal living even for young radicals devoted to the communal ideal.

---

[35] Daniel B. Reibel, Letter in *New York Times Magazine*, March 9, 1969, p. 19.

[36] Kingsley Widmer, "Thrust of the Underculture," *The Nation*, Dec. 30, 1968, pp. 716, 718.

PSYCHOLOGICAL COUNSELING OF STUDENTS

by

William Gerber

1 9 7 0
Nov. 25

PSYCHOLOGICAL COUNSELING OF STUDENTS

T HE CHERISHED NOTION of carefree student days has fallen victim to the strife and discord that many American schools have experienced in recent years. While there is now a glimmer of hope that the worst has passed, it cannot be said that a mass of students suddenly has found peace of mind. Indeed, young people in college and even high school have been candidates for professional help in sorting out their troubling emotions. Psychological counseling is already found on many campuses, and it seems likely to become a permanent fixture in the academic world.

While the need for psychological counseling of students at college level and below is often quite obvious, there is no unanimity of opinion as to why the need is more visible today than only a decade ago. According to one view, the social temper of the times has planted deep doubts and uncertainties in the minds of students. In short, society is held accountable. Another view, usually conservative in tone, is that overly permissive child-rearing practices—supposedly fostered by Dr. Benjamin Spock—have produced an indulged and over-protected student who is frightened by realities and who resorts to infantile expressions of rage at a world which is not as nurturing as his home nest. In short, students—or their parents—are held accountable.

Whether or not this "spoiled brat" view of students has any basis in fact, it is clear that constituted authority—both collegiate and governmental—was unprepared to deal effectively with student activism in the 1960s. Although the existence of activist groups provided a kind of home for some students who in the past might have disappeared quietly into some private agony, the general uproar on campus denied the individual student a secure setting in which to wrestle with his problems.

In the fall of 1970, passivism seemed to have replaced activism as the dominant mood of college students. But serenity had not returned to American campuses. The change of feeling appeared, instead, to reflect dejection and rejection. Richard Pipes, head of the Russian Research Center at Harvard University, observed to Editorial Research Reports that students had discovered "that a riot in Harvard Square isn't going to change the world." Moreover, there was accumulating evidence that "youth culture," extolled by American society for a decade or more, had begun to lose its charm.

A recent bit of evidence was supplied in the November elections, when proposals to lower the voting age were defeated in most of the 14 states where the question was placed on the ballot.[1] Those students who the previous spring vowed to canvass for anti-war candidates turned apathetic by election day. How this new apathy and political impotence will affect the individual student's psyche is not at all clear as yet. But boredom and apathy have been noted as an underlying cause of some of the emotional and drug problems in schools, both at the college level and below.

Seymour Halleck, director of Student Health Psychiatry at the University of Wisconsin, in November 1969 described a type of student who, he said, was becoming "more and more familiar to psychiatrists who work with students." "He is not a social activist or alienated or a hippy," Halleck declared. "He might best be thought of as an unrelenting stylist—an individual whose life is dominated by the values of immediacy, relevance, social maneuverability, psychological mindedness and dissent." One week this student is "into poetry," the next week "into Marcuse," the third week "into painting." The poem or painting is never finished, Halleck said, and the book never read beyond the first few chapters. The stylist's complaint is of boredom and meaninglessness.[2]

The theme of boredom and apathy—and alienation—is heard also in high schools. Explaining why teen-agers take to drugs, Robert M. Sandoe, headmaster at Cranbrook, a private boys' school in the wealthy Detroit suburb of Bloomfield Hills, said: "Kids feel society-less...They don't have any role in society and they feel alienated."[3] Dr. Bruno Bettelheim, whose colleagues sometimes consider him the "counter

---

[1] See Congressional Quarterly *Weekly Report*, Nov. 6, 1970, p. 2768, and "Politics and Youth," *E.R.R.*, 1970 Vol. I, pp. 261-278.
[2] Seymour Halleck, "You Can Go To Hell With Style," *Psychology Today*, November 1969, p. 16.
[3] Quoted in *The Wall Street Journal*, Nov. 12, 1970.

Spock" or the "Dr. No of child-care authorities," contends that the adolescent is crying out for a manhood which is postponed, at great psychological cost, by the technical nature of a society that has dispensed with his services.

"The adolescent today is someone who is grown up but still not independent economically," Bettelheim said. "This leads to terrible psychological strains." Adolescence, he added, is not a physiological period in one's life, like puberty, but a culturally imposed age. "As a particular style of life, it can only be possible if young people are not part of the working force. Until 1900, almost nobody became adolescent because after the age of 14 or 15 he went to work."[4]

Scope and Severity of Students' Psychic Ills

The typical youth of 14 or 15 today is not only in school but will remain there for several more years—quite likely until he is well into his twenties. If his high school did not provide psychological counseling, the odds are that his college will. School officials have come to recognize psychological counseling as a necessary adjunct to education. About one-half of the students who enter college do not graduate. It is probable that many of them drop out "not because their basic equipment is faulty, but because emotional and adjustment problems keep them from realizing their full potential."[5]

Emotional problems of a high school or college student may stem from his view of society or from something as private as his sex urges, unrealistic parental expectations, or his low grades. The problems may be relatively slight or quite severe. At one extreme, a thousand or more American college students take their own lives each year—a rate of self-inflicted death that tends to run 50 per cent higher than among their age group in the general population. According to a recent study conducted on behalf of the National Association of Mental Health, suicide of a college-age youth is most likely to result from loneliness and alienation, not from academic pressures or drug use.[6]

Young people are not mentally sicker today than in past generations, according to Dr. Edward J. Hornick, a New York

---

[4] Quoted by David Dempsey, "Bruno Bettelheim is Dr. No," *The New York Times Magazine*, Jan. 11, 1970, pp. 108-109.

[5] Roger D. Osborn (Ohio State University health service), "Pre-Crisis Intervention," *Journal of School Health*, November 1968, p. 568.

[6] See "Anatomy of Suicide," *E.R.R.*, 1963 Vol. II, p. 720, and "Alienated Youth," *E.R.R.*, 1966 Vol. II, p. 747.

psychiatrist who formerly was psychiatric consultant to Sarah Lawrence College. Mentally disturbed youths are "just more visible today," he asserts. Visibility has to do both with the increasing number of youths[7] and the decreasing reluctance of persons to seek professional help for their emotional problems. "The subject is discussed as casually as a visit to the dentist," Enid Nemy of *The New York Times* has written. "Everyone either knows or has heard of an adolescent who is undergoing psychiatric treatment."[8] In this atmosphere, the stigma of consulting a "shrink" is fast fading from view.

Psychological Counseling Programs in Colleges

The campus psychological counseling center is a place where students are informed they can unburden themselves without fear of rebuke or ridicule. In a likely situation, a trained psychologist on duty will reassuringly greet the student who comes for help and will encourage him to talk freely.

At the next stage, whether in the first session or after many sessions, the psychologist will encourage the student to view his problems objectively and seek ways to begin solving them. Though the emphasis is always upon the responsibility of the student to solve his own problems, the psychologist uses a variety of techniques for helping him. The student may be set to work on a series of explicit tasks and small challenges which would lead him to a goal he had previously feared to approach. Or he may be pressed to confront, in some other way, the ambiguities and contradictions in his conflicts.

Whether the psychologist takes an active counseling role or a "hands-holding" approach, his essential role is to help the student in self-understanding, self-direction and self-appreciation. The student will detect whether the counselor's concern is real or feigned, a therapist has said. "He will sense and respond to our warmth or coldness, our real involvement or our facade, our immediacy or our remoteness....He will respond to anything of ourselves that we present—or to nothing of ourselves if that is what we are giving him."[9]

The number of colleges that offer psychological counseling is not known with any degree of precision. Some surveys

---

[7] The number of American teen-agers was 20 per cent greater in 1970 (26.5 million) than a decade earlier, according to Census Bureau estimates. Their rate of population growth far exceeded that of older age groups.

[8] Enid Nemy, *The New York Times*, Feb. 20, 1970.

[9] Alfred Benjamin (of Tel Aviv University, Israel), *The Helping Hand* (1969), pp. 53-54.

conducted in recent years indicate that psychological counseling is widespread. Frank A. Nugent and E. N. Pareis reported in January 1968 that among 785 American colleges which replied to their survey questions, 401 reported having campus counseling centers. The number of full-time counselors varied widely from school to school, as shown in the following table:[10]

Psychologists employed	Per cent of schools	Psychologists employed	Per cent of schools
More than 12	3	1 to 6	74
7 to 12	6	Less than 1 full-time	17

Later information compiled by the University of Maryland Counseling Center, on the basis of a survey of about 140 colleges and universities across the country, indicated that the typical large university with 10,000 students or more has about seven full-time counselors. At smaller universities and colleges, four full-time counselors were found to be a representative number. At the large institutions, five of the seven counselors were likely to be holders of Ph.D. degrees; at the smaller schools, only one of the four counselors was likely to have attained a doctoral degree.

If all counseling and mental health personnel available on a typical large campus are taken into account, there is believed to be about one "helping person" for every 1,415 students. At the smaller schools, the ratio is calculated to be about one to 1,100. These figures, however statistically accurate, may suggest a greater availability of counselors and other professional helpers at campus psychological counseling centers than actually exists. That is because there are schools with no psychological counseling services.

Extent of Counseling Below the College Level

Counseling is needed in secondary and primary schools fully as much as in colleges. Estimates as to the proportion of school-age children in the United States who are moderately or seriously maladjusted range from 10 to 50 per cent.[11] Educational administrators are virtually unanimous in believing that schools should provide counseling at no charge for pupils who need it. Teachers who sense that a deeply

---

[10] Frank A. Nugent and E. N. Pareis, "Survey of Present Policies and Practices in College Counseling Centers in the United States of America," *Journal of Counseling Psychology,* January 1968, pp. 94-96.

[11] Lester N. Downing, *Guidance and Counseling Services; An Introduction* (1968), p. 282. See also "Future of Psychiatry," *E.R.R.,* 1969 Vol. I, p. 139.

rooted problem is destroying a child's serenity are able to refer the child to a school psychologist—if available.

These in-house psychologists conduct schoolwide mental hygiene programs, administer and interpret tests of personality and ability, try to discover emotional barriers to learning in underachievers, and provide individual counseling. School psychologists surveyed in 26 middle-sized American cities in 1966 had the following educational qualifications:

Holders of Ph. D. degrees	15%	No study beyond M.A.	35%
Graduate work beyond		Holders of B.A. degrees	
M.A.	47%	only	3%

The salary ceiling was $7,000 a year for those with a bachelor of arts degree and $12,000 for those with a doctorate.[12]

Two-hundred-fifty is generally recommended as the optimum number of pupils for whom a counselor should be responsible. Only Rhode Island (296) and New Jersey (306) approached that figure in 1965, the last year for which statistics are available. Mississippi (1,513) and Alabama (1,445) had the highest ratios of pupils to counselors. Elementary schools in the United States that year had about 2,500 counselors.[13] For secondary schools, the number of counselors is considerably higher and the pupil-counselor ratio has gradually been decreasing. (See table, opposite page.)

Annabel Ferguson, director of pupil services in the public schools of Prince Georges County, Md., has estimated that 3 to 5 per cent of the youngsters in that school system, in both elementary and secondary grades, see school psychologists during the course of a year. In dealing with children's emotional problems, she said, "the classroom teacher is sort of the first line of defense" and the school psychologist is the second line.[14]

A special counseling program operated in four experimental schools in Cobb County (Marietta), Ga., was described in the March 1970 issue of *American Education* as providing services to 2,500 elementary school pupils—1,000 of them in the first and second grades. A counseling team, consisting of four

---

[12] See *School Psychological Services* (1968, edited by James F. Magary), pp. 43, 74.
[13] Bruce Shertzer and Shelley C. Stone, *Foundations of Counseling* (1968), pp. 116, 118-119.
[14] Quoted in the Washington *Sunday Star*, July 26, 1970.

SECONDARY SCHOOL COUNSELORS

Year	Full-time counselors	Students per counselor	Year	Full-time counselors	Students per counselor
1958-59	12,000	960	1963-64	29,273	520
1959-60	18,000	640	1964-65	31,000	507
1960-61	21,828	570	1965-66	34,500	490
1961-62	24,492	550	1966-67	36,200	450
1962-63	27,180	530	1967-68	38,000	440

SOURCE: Bruce Shertzer and Shelley C. Stone, *Foundations of Counseling* (1968), p. 117.

child-development specialists (one per school), teachers' aides and secretaries, seeks to realize a child's learning potential during his elementary school years through individualized learning programs. The team can draw on the support of a project director, two learning specialists, a psychologist and a psychometrist—the last a person trained in the psychological theory and technique of mental measurement. Emotional difficulty is not the only type of problem that the team tries to cope with.

As an example of the program's work, recounted in the magazine, a six-year-old boy attracted the attention of a child-development specialist because of his low IQ test score of 82. The specialist called in the psychologist, who soon concluded that the IQ score was inaccurate but noted that the boy had some weaknesses, particularly in the area of numbers and spatial relationships. The youngster was permitted to enter a regular first-grade class rather than one for children with severe weaknesses. But he was assigned to a special class in perceptual motor training for 30 minutes a day and to a tutorial reading program. This meant that in addition to being taught reading every day by his teacher, he would have 15 minutes a day of individual reading instruction by a teacher's aide. The boy showed improvement in both areas in a matter of weeks and was able to remain in a regular class.

William Glasser, the psychiatrist and author, contends that in the early years of school many pupils decide that they are failures—in classroom achievement, making friends, having fun, winning the respect of others. They drop out and, quite likely, get into trouble. "Successful children generally don't get into trouble," he said. On the other hand, "better than nine out of ten delinquents are school failures."[15] The young-

---

[15] Quoted in *U.S. News & World Report*, April 27, 1970, p. 42. Glasser is the author of *Reality Therapy* and *Schools Without Failure*.

ster who considers himself a failure reacts by becoming ag-
gressively hostile or by withdrawing into a world of unreality
—a state that is sometimes labeled "mental illness" or, in
less extreme form, characterized by depressive spells and by
physical ailments like ulcers and back pains.

Some of these youngsters overcome their afflictions, Glasser said. "Others can be helped by therapy," he added, "but
the answer is prevention—not patch-up." His thought· is in
line with those of many psychologists involved with school
children in the elementary grades: that if they can be helped
to overcome their problems at an early stage, the odds are
much greater that they will not be in need of "patching-up"
in later years.

Counseling Theory and Development

AN EARLY ADVOCATE of counseling school-age children
was Lightner Witmer, director of the University of Pennsylvania psychological laboratory around the turn of the century.
In his talks with children, Witmer tried to uncover non-intel-
lectual barriers to learning. William R. Harper, founder and
first president of the University of Chicago, said in 1905 that
schools should counsel every student, not just those who
were troubled: "There should be a diagnosis of each student,
in order to discover his capacities, his tastes...his weaknesses,
and his defects; and upon the basis of such a diagnosis his
course of study should be arranged."[16]

Frank Parsons organized a bureau in Boston in 1908 for ad-
vising young people about preparing for their life's calling.
Though outside the school system, Parsons' bureau was a
forerunner of the secondary school vocational guidance programs. From these programs psychological counseling evolved.
Others who contributed to the theory and practice of psychological counseling in school included William Healey, who
in 1910 established a Juvenile Psychopathic Institute in
Chicago, and Arnold L. Gesell, founder in 1911 of a psychological clinic for children which became the Yale Clinic of
Child Development.

---

[16] William R. Harper, *The Trend in Higher Education* (1905), p. 94.

When Witmer and others were laying the foundations of psychological counseling, some of the better schools were beginning to take responsibility for providing personal guidance to their students—but not on emotional problems. On the genesis of school counseling programs, one study states: "Counseling may have begun in 1898 when Jesse B. Davis began work as a counselor at Central High School in Detroit, Michigan. For 10 years he helped students with educational and vocational problems."[17]

Establishment of Guidance Programs in Schools

It became apparent, after some years, that educational administrators needed to concern themselves more fully with counseling students who were hindered in their learning by maladjustment. Chicago was the first major city in which the authorities undertook to deal systematically with special learning difficulties. The Chicago board of education on Sept. 6, 1899, established a department of child study and pedagogical investigation. The new department was intended primarily to study problems of learning. As an adjunct of that function, it was charged with the duty of consulting individual students about lower-than-expected performance.

Guidance programs were developing slowly elsewhere also. Alfred Binet in 1905 established a pedagogical laboratory in a Paris elementary school where he experimented with teaching methods, including those aimed at dealing with learning difficulties. The London city council in 1913 appointed Cyril (later Sir Cyril) Burt as director of a psychological service in the board of education. This new service encouraged personal counseling in local schools. In Seattle, where various high schools had conducted counseling on differing and sometimes conflicting bases, the city board of education in 1913 organized a guidance bureau to coordinate and supervise this work in conformity with a set of consistent principles.

Guidance programs sprang up during the 1920s in public secondary schools in all parts of the United States. Vocational guidance often was the core of the programs, but talking with students about their personal problems came to be regarded as a legitimate part of the guidance counselor's job. Counseling systems began to appear in colleges also. Dr. Karl Menninger in 1920 helped to institute such a system at Washburn College in Topeka, Kan. Psychological counseling was

---

[17] Bruce Shertzer and Shelley C. Stone, *op. cit.*, p. 29.

begun in the early 1920s at Dartmouth, Vassar, Yale, and the U.S. Military Academy. By 1928, at least 16 colleges had student counseling programs.

Two main organizations of psychologists who specialize in counseling were formed after World War II. They were Division 16, School Psychology, founded in 1947 by the American Psychological Association, and the American Personnel and Guidance Association, established in 1952 by smaller existing societies. Today the American Psychological Association also sponsors Division 17, Counseling Psychology, and Division 12, Clinical Psychology, many of whose members are directly engaged in counseling students.

The profession of counselor has received a major boost from Congress in recent years. The National Defense Education Act of 1958 and its 1964 amendments "probably did as much as any one thing to expand the counseling and guidance field."[18] The 1958 act was aimed at strengthening sciences, mathematics and foreign languages—a response to Russian advances in science and particularly to the Soviet launching of Sputnik, the first earth satellite, Oct. 4, 1957.

One section of the act authorized federal money for guidance programs in public high schools that met standards to be set by the U.S. Commissioner of Education. In approving this section, lawmakers hoped that the capabilities of high school students could be identified early and developed fully. The act provided also for the commissioner to sign contracts with colleges for the training of guidance counselors. The 1964 amendments expanded federal support of guidance programs and extended the support to public elementary schools, junior colleges, and private schools.

Emergence of Diverse Theories on Counseling

Practitioners of counseling in schools and colleges, as they increased in numbers, began to be differentiated according to the slogans and techniques which they preferred. Slogans flowered into theories, and techniques into creeds. Counseling fads came and went. The earliest of the formulated viewpoints on counseling was the non-directive approach, also termed client-centered counseling, developed by psychologist Carl R. Rogers.[19] Advocates of this system sometimes invoke,

---

[18] Joseph W. Hollis and Lucile U. Hollis, *Personalizing Information Processes; Educational, Occupational, and Personal-Social* (1969), p. 26.

[19] Carl R. Rogers, *Counseling and Psychotherapy* (1942) and *Client-Centered Therapy* (1951).

TYPES OF COUNSELING THERAPISTS

Psychiatrist. A doctor of medicine who specializes in treatment of emotional problems and mental illness, whether by individual or group methods and whether by psychological or physiological means.

Psychoanalyst. A psychiatrist who uses psychoanalysis as the principal approach to emotional problems.

Clinical psychologist. A person without an M.D. degree, though often with the degree of Ph.D. in psychology, who is qualified to employ psychological methods but not to prescribe drugs.

---

as a substructure for their methods, the child-centered educational theories of John Dewey.

In the non-directive approach, the counselor serves mainly as a sounding board, while the troubled student is expected to gain relief at once and self-understanding later by uninhibitedly expressing what he feels. This approach has been criticized on the ground that if the student is allowed to "ventilate" excessively, he may feel so good that he will not bother to go on to the causes of his difficulties.

In the directive approach, by contrast, the counselor does much of the talking. He dominates each counseling session. He conveys diagnostic findings, offers interpretations, asks leading questions, gives advice, and persuades. This approach received support from the psychiatric system called logotherapy (reasoning therapy), developed during World War II by Viktor E. Frankl, an Austrian. In logotherapy, the counselor reasons with the patient in an effort to convince him that his vague fears are groundless.

Behavioral therapy, which currently is in vogue, represents an attempt to apply some of the principles of learning that have been discovered by experimental psychologists in studies with both humans and animals. Attention is given to what actually is happening in the student's life, not what he thinks or fears *might* happen. Thus, instead of talking and reasoning about why a student might fear and avoid talking with people, the behavior therapist endeavors to teach the student such things as how to begin a conversation, how to make small talk at parties, and how to determine when a person is becoming bored with the conversation.

In learning to talk with people more easily, the student often discovers that he really is not afraid of people or he learns what it is that he is afraid of. In the latter case, the behavior therapist may help the student to overcome the fear

173

if it is an unrealistic one, or teach him to avoid the situation if the fear is realistic. Some behaviorally oriented counseling centers are able to provide legal assistance if the student is involved in stress-provoking problems, say with a recalcitrant landlord or perhaps in a separation-divorce proceeding—cases in which the student wants to assume responsibility for himself instead of turning to his parents.

Psychoanalytic counseling, especially in the form sponsored by Rollo May, a professor of psychology at New York University, lays stress on the revelational character of an encounter of one person with another as taught in general, non-psychiatric terms by Paul J. Tillich and Martin Buber. Tillich (1886-1965), a German-born American Protestant theologian and professor, in his writings and teaching helped many to clarify the meaning of the Christian faith in relation to the needs and dilemmas of modern man; Buber (1878-1965), a Jewish philosopher, in *I and Thou* (1937) and other works expounded a personalist philosophy of God, man and society that profoundly influenced contemporary thought, including Christian theology.

In another counseling system that is currently prominent, that of relationship therapy, the focus is not on what has happened to the student in the past, but on his present relations with the therapist. The question which is uppermost in the counseling sessions is: How can the client use the therapist? The answer depends on what the student needs and how the therapist can help him to get what he needs.

Inconclusive Evaluation of Counseling Practices

Group counseling also is being tried in some colleges. Its advantages are that it saves time by helping several students at once and it enables a perplexed student to express his misgivings in a permissive atmosphere and in the presence of his peers. It often has a catalytic effect in that one student, seeing others try to change themselves, is motivated to do so himself. Techniques of group counseling include the psychodrama, in which individuals act out personal experiences while others comment, and the sociodrama, in which members of the group play changing roles in acting out experiences which have caused them grief.

No one seems to know to what extent students have benefited from psychological counseling. Ohio State University, seeking to determine the effectiveness of the university's counselors, studied the record of (1) students who, on the basis of personality tests, had received counseling, and (2) students who had similar test scores but, because of a staff shortage, had not been counseled.

The study showed that those who had been counseled stayed in college longer, transferred less from college to college, received fewer failing grades, and made fewer visits to the university health services for physical problems. However, the university official who made the comparison offered only a moderately affirmative conclusion regarding the value of the counseling program: "It may very well be that the reaching out process says to a new student that he is more than a number and a statistical data card. It may say that even a large, seemingly impersonal university *does* care about its students."[20]

The University of Minnesota studied, after 25 years, approximately 400 individuals who had been counseled during their student days at the university in the 1930s, and the same number of their contemporaries who had made similar scores on college entrance examinations but who had not received counseling while they were students. David P. Campbell, who conducted this study, reported on it in qualified terms as follows:

> *First,* these data indicate a very mild difference in achievement between counseled and non-counseled students 25 years later, especially among the men. Although the differences on the specific criteria of achievement were not large and often not statistically significant, they were consistently in favor of the counseled students.
>
> *Second,* the data supported the general conclusion that counseling did indeed exert a beneficial effect on the student's achievement. This effect was most apparent on immediate criteria such as grades and graduation, but, although it withered considerably, the impact did not completely disappear over 25 years.[21]

A group of psychologists at Kent State University in Ohio reviewed the scholarly literature on the effectiveness of psychological counseling of students. They came away skeptical of beneficial claims. "Those involved in counseling usually have no way of knowing whether their efforts result in 'success' because of counseling, in spite of counseling, or because what-

---

[20] Roger D. Osborn, *op. cit.,* p. 573.
[21] David P. Campbell, "Achievements of Counseled and Non-Counseled Students Twenty-five Years After Counseling," in *Research in Counseling* (1968), p. 402.

ever environmental stresses produced the initial problem were removed."[22]

Frank A. Nugent, professor of psychology and director of the counseling center at Western Washington State College at Bellingham, noted that considerable numbers of students, regardless of their political orientation, doubt the value of counseling:

> Some campus ultra-liberals tend to believe that psychologists encroach upon the individual's rights in their attempts to adjust everyone to a social norm, while ultra-conservatives consider therapy or counseling a form of brainwashing with a subversive tinge. Of the remainder...a considerable number are apprehensive about the perceptive and manipulative power of psychologists and have at best mixed feelings about unveiling themselves to "head shrinkers."[23]

In addition to student doubts, another factor raises questions about the effectiveness of psychological counseling. Some studies of mental illness in all age groups indicate that two-thirds of those who receive psychiatric treatment show improvement, and approximately the same proportion of those who do not receive treatment also show improvement.

On the other hand, two authors who recently reviewed 101 research studies found evidence of positive effects of counseling in about 80 per cent of the studies. These studies covered a broad range of individual and group therapy practices involving patients of all ages and differing severity of problems. The authors were careful to note that their findings did not unequivocally establish the efficacy of all counseling efforts with all kinds of problems. They did state that "controlled research has been notably successful in demonstrating significantly more behavioral change in treated patients than in untreated controls." "In general, the better the quality of the research, the more positive the results obtained."[24]

Dr. David A. Hills of Wake Forest University Center for Psychological Services suggests that "we are dealing with a very slippery notion when we talk about 'improvement' as a result of counseling." "Many people recover from physical illness without benefit of medical attention," he told Editorial Research Reports. "But most people feel that their

---

[22] Lawrence Litwack and others, introduction to Chapter 7, "Evaluation of Counseling Effectiveness," in *Research in Counseling* (1968), p. 338.

[23] Frank A. Nugent, "Confidentiality in College Counseling Centers," *Personnel and Guidance Journal*, May 1969, p. 875.

[24] J. Meltzoff and M. Kornreich, *Research in Psychotherapy* (1970), p. 177.

chances of recovery without...disfiguring scars, systemic weaknesses, or predispositions to subsequent infection are better if medical consultation has been available during the recovery process.

"It seems to many of us in counseling that the individual with problems has a better chance of discovering effective, growth-promoting solutions if there is an opportunity to work out these problems with a professional counselor. After all, most people gain some relief—that is, show 'improvement'— if they bury, deny, or run away from their problems. And most people ultimately discover that this solution by denial or escape eventually leaves them bent out of shape in some important way."

Directions of Psychological Guidance

HELP FOR STUDENTS with emotional problems will develop in the coming years along lines which are beginning to be foreshadowed. Awareness of a need for enlarged counseling staffs seems to be growing, but financial stringency may inhibit their growth. One approach that has recently come into prominence involves widespread use of drug therapy in elementary schools.

That a "drug culture" flourishes in American schools, from junior high on up, is well known. What came as a surprise to many people in 1970, however, was that in some schools "behavior modification drugs" were being prescribed under the auspices of school authorities to calm unruly young children and help them learn. Robert C. Maynard of *The Washington Post* reported in July that 3,000 to 6,000 youngsters in the Omaha public schools were receiving stimulants, including amphetamines ("pep pills"), to counteract hyperkinesis—the so-called "hyperactive child" syndrome. These stimulants were said to have the reverse effect on children from what they do on adults, calming them down rather than pepping them up.

It soon became known that similar practices were followed, on the advice of medical doctors, in several school systems throughout the country. Rep. Cornelius E. Gallagher (D N.J.), a leading congressional advocate of "right to privacy," attacked the practices in a series of House speeches and demanded to know if federal funds were involved in these drug-dispensing programs. As it turned out, federal grants, made available through the National Institutes of Health, subsidized a number of projects involving research into the effect of drugs on "hyperactive" children.

In most of the research projects, the National Institutes of Health underwrote the cost of a medical team, composed of a pediatrician and a psychiatrist, which worked with local schools. If the parents of the unruly child approved, he was prescribed a stimulant drug, and his progress—if any—charted. Medical treatment is usually prescribed over a course of years, at least until the child reaches his early teens. As yet, the returns are not all in. In the interim, medical opinion varies as to the usefulness of drugs as an aid to learning. Dr. Byron B. Oberst, an Omaha pediatrician active in working with hypertense children, has said a drug will "help some children with a learning disability while it does not help others." Dr. Sidney Adler, a neurological pediatrician in Anaheim, Calif., said that by prescribing drugs to treat children with learning disabilities, "I have saved many, many kids from going down the drain."[25]

The use of drugs as an aid to learning—and hence as an adjunct to psychological counseling—is not likely to fade from view. *Today's Education,* journal of the National Education Association, reported in January 1969: "Biochemical and psychological mediation of learning is likely to increase. New drama will play on the education stage as drugs are introduced experimentally to improve in the learner such qualities as personality, concentration and memory."

Student Testing to Determine Emotional Stability

School and college counseling services in the future probably will devote more attention than they have in the past to the prevention of incapacitating tensions among students. Prevention is not only more desirable, but often cheaper, than cure. Instruction in mental hygiene already is widespread in elementary and secondary schools. Courses in sex education, especially those in secondary schools, are emphasizing the avoidance of heartbreak and other psychological traps of boy-girl relations.

---

[25] Oberst and Adler quoted in *U.S. News & World Report,* July 13, 1970, p. 49.

In colleges, orientation programs try to ease student distress. Many colleges include personality questions in psychological tests administered to freshmen. In the California junior colleges, a counselor goes over the test results with each student, discussing strong and weak points in the student's mental makeup and any indicated elements of emotional instability. If the test scores show a need for professional guidance, the counselor may refer the student to the counseling center.

At Ohio State University, tests given to all newcomers include questions such as "Do you often wish you were dead and away from it all?" Students with abnormal scores on such questions are invited to confer with psychologists at the university health service. Roger D. Osborn noted that "Ohio State has far fewer suicides than would be expected based on national student averages." Frank A. Nugent wrote that "counseling centers can be a constructive resource when administrators and faculty committees try to set up fair and psychologically sound policies about drugs, demonstrations, disciplinary procedures, and selective procedures."

Expansion of Staffs at Campus Counseling Centers

To help future students cope with their problems, psychological counseling staffs will have to be enlarged. As projected by one source,[26] and shown in the following table, twice as many counselors will be needed in 1975 as were available 10 years earlier.

	1965	1970	1975
Four-year colleges	4,000	6,674	7,591
Junior colleges	791	4,000	5,000
Public secondary schools	31,000	44,938	71,887

The demand for psychological counselors in colleges and universities has been high in recent years, but the fiscal situation in these institutions is becoming stringent. Some observers predict that counseling will feel the belt-tightening before academic instruction does.

While administrators may value psychological counseling highly, many of them are careful not to identify closely with the campus counseling center. Students tend to regard the administration as the Establishment—a dirty word in their

[26] John F. McGowan (ed.), *Counselor Development in American Society* (1965), p. 109.

current lexicon. Prof. Nugent has written that counseling centers closely associated with college authorities are objects of particular suspicion because "40 per cent of the counseling center directors have apparently violated the code of ethics" regarding the confidentiality of talks with students. Records of counseling sessions have been made available to the dean of students, disciplinary officers, the Peace Corps, and prospective business employers.[27] Students seem to appreciate being able to consult someone who is only a little older than they are and who does not represent the university administration. Dormitory counselors and adult advisers in fraternity houses sometimes provide convenient sounding boards. The role of these counselors is complicated, however, by their responsibility for discipline. When a frustrated student breaks up the furniture, it may be hard for the counselor to keep his equanimity.

It is no part of the counselor's job to provide pat answers to basic questions. He does not make the student try to accept the current values of society. Rather, he seeks to help the student find answers for himself. A counselor can serve as a friendly foil for a student who is working out his general beliefs about man and the world, good and evil, the temporal and the eternal. In some cases, religious beliefs are basic to the student's philosophy of life; in others, ultimate questions about eternity and infinity are brushed aside.

For religious and non-religious students alike, a major part of their philosophy of life is their scheme of values—that is, their understanding of what considerations outweigh what others in making judgments and decisions. To young people striving to bring a value structure to birth, a counselor—like Socrates—can serve as a psychological midwife.

---

[27] Frank A. Nugent, *op. cit.,* p. 878.